Circle of

SUNY series in the Anthropology of Work
June C. Nash, editor

and

SUNY series in Anthropological Studies of Contemporary Issues
Jack R. Rollwagen, editor

Circle of Goods

Women, Work, and Welfare
in a Reservation Community

Tressa Berman

State University of New York Press

Published by
State University of New York Press, Albany

© 2003 State University of New York

For information, address State University of New York Press,
90 State Street, Suite 700, Albany, NY 12207

Production by Judith Block
Marketing by Patrick Durocher

Library of Congress Cataloging-in-Publication Data

Berman, Tressa Lynn.
  Circle of goods : women, work, and welfare in a reservation community /
Tressa Berman.
      p. cm.—(SUNY series in the anthropology of work) (SUNY series in
  anthropological studies of contemporary issues)
  Includes bibliographical references and index.
  ISBN 0-7914-5535-1 (alk. paper)—ISBN 0-7914-5536-X (pbk. : alk. paper)
    1. Mandan women—North Dakota—Fort Berthold Indian Reservation—Social conditions.
  2. Hidatsa women—North Dakota—Fort Berthold Indian Reservation—Social conditions.
  3. Indians of North America—North Dakota—Fort Berthold Indian Reservation—
  Government relations.   4. Indians of North America—Public welfare—North Dakota—Fort
  Berthold Indian Reservation.   5. Public welfare—Government policy—North Dakota—
  North Dakota—Fort Berthold Indian Reservation.   6. Fort Berthold Indian Reservation
  (N.D.)—Economic conditions.   7. Fort Berthold Indian Reservation (N.D.)—Social
  conditions. I. Title. II. Series. III. Series: SUNY series in anthropological studies of
  contemporary issues.

E99.M2 B37 2003
305.897'520784—dc21
                                                                                    2002029233

10 9 8 7 6 5 4 3 2

Contents

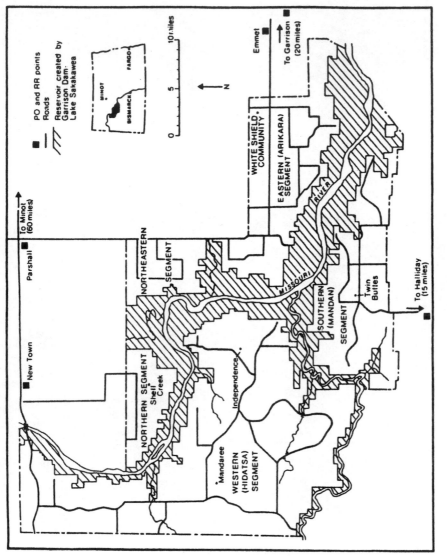

Map 1. Fort Berthold Indian Reservation.

Illustrations

Acknowledgments

I acknowledge the following friends, colleagues, and tribal officials for their help, support, and willingness to let an "outsider" come in. By thanking the following individuals, I neither imply their participation in the research, nor their endorsement of my interpretations, conclusions, perceptions, or the existence of a book at all. Nonetheless, in helping me as a human being, I am a better person for it. I hope this book, in some small way, can be of use to the people of Fort Berthold and beyond. My heartfelt thanks to all the women who contributed to this book, and who I did not name out of respect for their anonymity. I am grateful to them nonetheless.

For guidance through the circle and for comfort from the North Dakota storms: Birdie Chase and the sisters of "Ree row"; Iva Goodbird and Peter Deane; Lucy Rosario and family; my guardian angel Caroline Pleets Chase; Alvina Hall and family; Mary Elk; Joane Mandan; Rosemarie Mandan; Doreen Yellow Bird; Rusty and JoEsther Parshall; Tillie Walker; Rose Crow Flies High (in memoriam); Grace Henry; Orville Mandan; Keith Bear; Sammie Little Owl; and the late Herbert Wilson, M.D. My gratitude to Charlene and Loren ("Sonny") Fredericks for all the years and all the love.

For institutional assistance: Former Tribal Chair Wilbur Wilkinson; Former State Commissioner of Indian Affairs Debbie Painte; Quincy Baker, and the staff of the Fort Berthold Community College; Pete Coffey Jr. and the staff of KMHA radio; Marilyn Hudson and the Four Bears Museum; the Fort Berthold Housing Authority; Tribal Administration personnel; JTPA, TERO, and BIA offices; the curatorial and library staff of the North Dakota State Heritage Center and the archival staff at the Minnesota Historical Society.

Thanks to my friends in Bismarck who fed me and talked to me about wild rice, sunflowers, and other things that matter. Gary and Sharon of the Green Earth Café; Terry Wiklund; and Jennifer and Wes Jones.

For financial support: American Cultures Fellowship, the University of California at Los Angeles American Indian Research Center; American Philosophical Society; and Judy Bick for the "Georgia Fellowship," which made possible three months of writing time in Berkeley. Thanks to Dr. JoAllyn Archambault, National Museum of Natural History, Smithsonian Institution, Dr. Bea Medicine, and Professors Luis Kemnitzer and June Nash, all wise mentors. Many thanks to my research assistants who continued to move the work along every time I moved: Glenda George, Terri Place, and Senta Gorrie. Thanks to my colleagues at Arizona State University West for advice on the publishing trade and for the opportunities to present early versions of the manuscript. For assistance with photo reproductions, Photo Concepts of Phoenix, Arizona, and Laree Bates, archivist, Heard Museum, Phoenix, Arizona, and Sharon Silengo, Photo Archivist, State Historical Society of North Dakota. Thanks to Michael Rinella, my careful editor at SUNY Press. Thanks also to Ruth Weine. For institutional support in providing a place to put it all together: the Women's Leadership Institute at Mills College and the Department of Anthropology, California Academy of Sciences. For editorial input and spirited friendship, Massimiliano (Max) Carocci.

And not least, my parents: Judith Batemen-Bick, and Gene and Lisa Berman.

Proceeds from the sale of this book will be donated to the Fort Berthold Community College with the hope of inspiring a new generation of scholars.

Permissions

Chapter 1, excerpt from *Reservation Blues*, by Sherman Alexie. Copyright 1995, Grove/Atlantic, Inc. Used with permission. Chapter 2, excerpt reprinted from "The Community as Worksite: American Indian Women's Artistic Production," by Tressa Berman, in *More Than Class, Studying Power in U.S. Workplaces*, pp. 73–95, Ann E. Kingsolver, editor, © 1998 State University of New York Press. Used with permission. Chapter 2, epigraph quoted with courtesy permission of the author © 1973 by Alice Walker. Chapter 3, excerpts reprinted from "Bringing it to the Center: Artistic Production as Economic Development Among American Indian Women of Fort Berthold, North Dakota" in *Research in Human Capital and Development. American Indian Economic Development*, Volume 10, Alan Sorkin, Carol Ward and C. Matthew Snipp, volume editors, pp. 171–189, © 1996 with permission from Elsevier Science. Chapter 4, epigraph reprinted from *Custer Died For Your Sins: An Indian Manifesto* by Vine Deloria,

Jr., Copyright © 1969 by Vine Deloria, Jr.; courtesy permission, Vine Deloria, Jr. Chapter 5, Epigraph reproduced from *Woman Native Other* by T. Minh-Ha Trinh, © 1989 by Indiana University Press. Used with permission.

Preface, for permission to reprint map of Fort Berthold, *Cultural Survival Quarterly, Inc.* Chapter 1, Figure [1.1] #603A, Dancing Bull Ration Ticket, 2nd quarter 1902, State Historical Society of North Dakota; Chapter 2, Figure [2.1] #41-278, Kate (Hopkins) Star, Daughter Theresa, State Historical Society of North Dakota; Figure [2.4], Eagle Woman Photo, LXXV, Box 142.G.10.6F-1, Gilbert L. and Frederick N. Wilson Papers, Minnesota Historical Society and American Museum of Natural History Library. Chapter 4, Figure [4.2] National Welfare Rights Organization, 1968 Poor Peoples March, Washington, D.C., photo by Bernie Boston, Used with permission.

Cover photo: Jesse at Armstrong (Lining up for rations at Fort Berthold) 1897, 41–465, State Historical Society of North Dakota.

Preface

[Collections] of "facts and images which I refused to exploit by letting my imagination work on them; in other words, the negation of a novel. To reject all fables . . . nothing but these facts all these facts." (1946, 156)

From the start, writing this journal, I've struggled against a poison: the idea of publication." (1934, 215)

Michel Leiris as cited in James Clifford,
The Predicament of Culture

Writing an ethnography requires a complex set of dialogues, those realized over the course of months and years of field work, the internal narratives that sit on the writer's shoulder, or those that seem to peer out from within stacked boxes of papers, transcripts, and books.

Clifford Geertz (1988) illuminated the task of anthropologists: they write. But more significantly, they listen. These conversations—engaged, imagined, and overheard—take shape among voices in the field, one's self, and a potential audience. This book is a distillation of those voices, converging in more than ten years of association among the people of Fort Berthold reservation in North Dakota.

The Mandan, Hidatsa, and Arikara (Sáhnish) comprise the Three Affiliated Tribes, a federally recognized tribal government with all the contradictions of "limited sovereignty" that such a status confers. Not all Indigenous peoples of North America agreed to federally chartered governments (via the Indian Reorganization Act of 1934), nor do all tribes have the status conveyed by federal recognition (treaty rights, federal-trust relations). This book is an argument neither for nor against such interventions, but begins from the premise that federal-trust, as a bundle of fiduciary and regulatory rights, obligates the federal government to American Indian Tribes.[1] Taken as a whole, these policies form the corpus of Federal Indian Law, first enacted as a set of international rights that establish American Indian Tribes as "domestic dependent" nations.[2]

I did not set out to write a book about policy; nor as the selection from Leiris cited in the epigraph suggests, did I set out to write a book at all. I had hoped to compile a series of testimonies about work that would illuminate, in some small way, American Indian women's own conceptions about what work means to them. I had already considered the informal economy as an unrecognized form of women's labor and had decided not to write about ceremonial life. Nonetheless, my participation in all the rounds of daily life, including ceremonies, qualifies me to write about the impact of federal policy on the reservation economy better than if I had not lived in the community at all. As the chapters of this book show, the time and energy spent preparing for ceremonial events figure highly into informal economic strategies. By describing the daily rounds without divulging ceremonial rites, I hope to show how policy makers can respect the needs of reservation communities by illuminating how subsistence envelopes all aspects of social life, alimentary as well as cultural.

The year I finished my dissertation, the United States was increasingly testing ideas about welfare reform in attempts to revamp and reapportion welfare benefits nationwide. However, the restructuring of welfare programs that followed the Personal Responsibility and Work Opportunity Reconciliation Act of 1996 (PL 104–193) was little more than a dismantling of welfare as we knew it. The effects of welfare reform have already had an impact in Indian Country, and future unforeseen effects will no doubt continue to be felt. The one that concerned me most as the act went into effect was the way in which the legislation appeared to dismiss long-held treaty rights, especially by giving increasing powers to states, thereby ignoring the historical basis for federal-trust (cf. O'Brien 2000).

Because my field research focused on the intersection of kinship, economic development, and the informal economy of American Indian women, I wagered that welfare reform—targeted largely at women and children—would have additional unforeseen consequences on these areas of reservation life. Again, I was brought back to my original goal: to highlight the voices of Fort Berthold women's work lives, but now with a greater purpose to serve; one that would show how the effects of welfare reform can potentially interrupt the dialogue of community life. I position myself within that conversation, which I began more than ten years ago as a guest in the homes of my Fort Berthold friends and family.

The Road to Fort Berthold.

I began my forays to Fort Berthold as a graduate student undertaking museum studies at the University of Colorado Museum, where more than 250 objects from the Fort Berthold reservation reside.[3] Always restless among archives and collection bins, I proposed a field trip that would take me to North Dakota to contextualize the historic collection of moccasins, knife sheaths, bags, dolls, drums, and garments from two generations of reservation life. The historic period of the collection spanned the 1920s to the 1960s, but focused primarily on the symbols of Mandan, Hidatsa, and Arikara life prior to the 1951 building of the Garrison Dam—the overwhelming swell of water that would submerge a way of life forever.

When I first arrived at Fort Berthold, I knew no one. I had a few contacts from colleagues, and these were mostly linguists who had worked intensively with several individuals over many years. These introductions proved invaluable and enabled me to make the transition from "stranger" to "friend"[4] with as much ease as any outsider could hope to have. What drove me was the conviction that museum collections cannot stand apart from their makers, nor can their significance be fully understood without accounting for the cultural and historical changes that inspired them. Motivated by the deconstructionist movement in museum studies (e.g., Karp and Lavine 1991), I visited around with my slides and catalogue cards, but as one sage advisor pointed out: anthropology is always about something else. And so the stories that the objects uncovered led me to settle on the task of showing how art production, kinship, economy, and identity become intertwined variables that wrap themselves around policy in ever-adaptable ways.

Some notes on the format of this book: More than five years of fieldwork culminated in a series of taped interviews, all open-ended and conversational, but drawing consistently on similar domains of work, family, economy, land rights, and kinship. The voices of the women featured here derive directly from those transcripts, and I acknowledge the invisible, yet heavy-handed role of editor that I play. For reasons we agreed on prior to interview sessions, all names have been changed to ensure anonymity, except in cases of public notoriety, where I draw from public records such as newspapers, radio, conferences, public transcripts, or other previously published work. The ethnographies of Alfred Bowers, who made a lifelong and systematic study of Mandan and Hidatsa kinship and ceremonial life (1950 and 1965, respectively) are cited here generously to affirm the continuity of these complex systems from a contemporary standpoint, as well as to avoid duplicating his copious body of work.

My early work at Fort Berthold involved me more deeply in Mandan and Hidatsa life. I was ritually adopted by a Mandan-Hidatsa-Arikara family whose primary identification was Mandan and Hidatsa and who collectively spoke three languages. My adoptive mother was a Mandan speaker and had received several community achievement awards for her assistance to linguists in constructing Mandan grammar and dictionaries. The work of the late Bob Hollow, a linguist who worked carefully and tirelessly to transcribe the language, assisted me more than he will have the chance to know. My adoptive parents likewise took him as a "son," and so he was also my brother. Having come to Fort Berthold from Sioux Country with some knowledge of the Lakota language, I settled on the Hidatsa language (also of Siouan stock), over which I spent countless hours attempting the nuanced speech that never easily, and nowhere fluently, struggled to free itself from my tongue.

My associations with Arikaras came later and more slowly. Some of this I attribute to their generalized distance between the Mandan and Hidatsa and my relationships with them. Historically, Mandans and Hidatsas, although they have distinct languages and cultural histories, have always shared more in common with each other than with neighboring Arikaras, who were the last to join them at Like-A-Fishhook Village in the 1860s. By then, the Mandans already had been decimated twice by smallpox and had intimately merged with the Hidatsas in both social and ceremonial life. Furthermore, their languages share a common linguistic family (Siouan), whereas the Arikara language descends from Caddoan. When the Fort Berthold reservation was first established in 1864, the Arikaras settled on the far eastern edge, where their primary community exists to this day. After the displacement caused by the Garrison Dam, the Hidatsas and Mandans were further separated on discrete segments of the reservation. The western-most Hidatsa territory abuts the rugged badlands and has offered itself as cattle country ever since the Indian Reorganization era first introduced the grass-eating bovines to the reservation economy—although they could never replace what was lost in majesty, prestige, and subsistence economy with the slaughter of the buffalo.

In writing this book, several predecessors naturally came to mind, as the ghosts of writers past will do when they rise and fall on the conscience to remind, critique, and inspire. In this vein, I was reminded of Loretta Fowler's (1987) work among the Arapahoes and Gros Ventres, and how I admired her honesty for the difficulty in representing a balanced tribal perspective. Other "foremothers" include Margery Wolf (1992), whose *A Thrice-Told Tale* first set down for me the possibility of writing a narrative structure in anthropology that embodied more than one voice in an important move away from authoritarian master narratives. Later, I decided that a "truer" text must necessarily be multivocal and that one way to highlight this was to give various typesets to polyphonous speakers. This explains the ways I have offset not only Fort Berthold women's testimonies, but also those composite accounts I draw from the collection of my own experiences. Anna Tsing (1993) showed the success of this type of approach in her book *In the Realm of the Diamond Queen*, and I thank her in hindsight for doing so because, regrettably, I read this important work only after landing on my own narrative structure.

The title of this book brings together several inseparable themes: (1) that the circulation of goods serves as a symbolic system of social and power relations; (2) that women stand at the center of community relations; and (3) that the dimensions of work, family, creativity, and ritual passages serve as intersections within the circle of life. As introduced in chapter 1, and highlighted throughout this book, much of Fort Berthold women's lives and my own time among them was spent provisioning the daily round.

Many of the women I assisted, elders in particular, received commodity food as part of their government assistance packages. I went on frequent forays to commodity warehouse distribution centers and learned, the hard way, the difference between making fry bread with store-bought versus government-issued flour. Stories of the necessary evils of commodity foods run like water through reservation narratives, mixing with this and that, from jokes to food shortages. One distribution period will be well remembered as the summer of Desert Storm fry bread in reference to the apparent surplus of flour and bread mix sent back (although some say rejected) from U.S. Army personnel stationed overseas during the Gulf War. Women joked that fry bread made with this mix had a texture comparable to the artillery used in the war. Thus, when posing for a photo, as I often asked people to do, the cant to "say commodity cheese!" rises replete with double entendre, capturing the knowing smiles, and finding that even at the heart of struggle lies an affirming sense of humor. If nothing else, I have learned this.

Chapter 1

"Say Commodity Cheese!"

Thomas was not surprised by Victor's sudden violence. These little wars were inti-mate affairs for those who dreamed in childhood of fishing for salmon but woke up as adults to shop at the Trading Post and stand in line for USDA commodity food in-stead. They savagely, repeatedly, opened up cans of commodities and wept over the rancid meat, forced to eat what stray dogs ignored.

Sherman Alexie, *Reservation Blues*

This book is about the way federal policy has repeatedly targeted American Indians through time, and the way American Indian women creatively resist outside efforts at ravaging their way of life. Beginning with treaties, and now through state welfare reform, American Indians have re-formed their families and communities to cope with social and economic constraints while fashioning new cultural meanings from the remnants of colonial intervention. Drawing from Spokane novelist Sherman Alexie's satirical description of reservation life, the snapshot of Thomas's and Victor's struggle over a can of commodity food symbolizes the residual effects of more than 150 years of structured dependency that began when the first parcel of Native American land was exchanged for ration tickets dispensed by government agents to obedient Indian subjects. The terms of surrender negotiated and codified by treaties specified the means of dispossession, which frequently involved payments to individual Indians "in lieu of the privilege [to build roads and military posts]."[1] With the final removal and relocation period of prereservation life, treaties became the tool for containing Native unrest, and as such, can be understood as the first policy pacts with American Indians.

1

Charlene, a Hidatsa elder whose grandparents were among the last settled on the Fort Berthold reservation in the late 1800s, recounted the terms of
resettlement as told to her:

> *At that time, the government gave stoves and furniture to these
> people. . . . They make a fire outside and cook and they [settled Indians]
> always laughed at them, [they'd say,] "they're poor, and us, we got a lot of
> money," like that. . . . When they [the Indians] got that per cap [govern-
> ment disbursement], they [the government] took some money back to pay
> for the commodities, to pay for the stove, the axe . . . so they [the govern-
> ment] didn't give it to them [the Indians], they paid for it!*

More than thirty years ago, Frances Fox Piven and Richard Clowen
(1971) convincingly argued that the expansion of welfare policies can be posi-
tively correlated to the state's need to contain social unrest. Following from their
argument, the expansion and contraction of American Indian welfare and federal
assistance programs can be viewed as extensions of federal policies to contain resistance to dispossession and assimilation (Deloria and Lytle 1984; Wilkins
1997; Wilkins and Lomawaima 2001). Since nineteenth-century treaties, American Indians continue to live within the most bureaucratic communities in the
United States—beginning at birth on receipt of a tribal enrollment number, the
symbol of the federal-trust subsumption of sovereignty that validates entitlement to government programs, such as annuities and housing subsidies.

This book examines the tensions between the kinds of policies that impact the reservation economy and the cultural commitments that maintain
community life on a reservation—specifically, among the Mandan, Hidatsa,
and Arikara of Fort Berthold, North Dakota. At Fort Berthold, the centrality
of women's roles as provisioners is underscored by matrilineality, which pre-
vails as the dominant mode of reckoning kin among all three tribes.[2] The persistence of matrilineal kinship arrangements likewise influences the ways that
matrifocal (i.e., woman-centered) contours of community relations flow. One
of the points I raise in this book is how structural inequalities that create matrifocal households can sometimes be masked by traditional matrilineal forms
of kinship arrangements. The descriptions of reservation life portrayed here
echo other reservation histories, and also, I expect, resonate with anyone who
has ever had to work for a living wage, look for adequate housing, or provide
one's family with food. For American Indian women, the daily ways of achiev-

ing these goals intertwine with the complex ways that kinship ties perpetuate ceremonial life.

Although ceremonial life is key to understanding how these tensions get worked out, this is not a book about ceremonies. My own partial understandings, partial truths (Haraway 1988) remain informed by my participation in all aspects of community life, including as an audience for the stories Fort Berthold women told me about their own approaches to work (Nirayan 1993; Rosaldo 1993). Together these stories form their own kind of oral history about work in a reservation community. By infusing Fort Berthold women's narratives with an analysis of the reservation economy, they lend their voice to the telling of the tale, and in this way, write themselves into the larger history of Indian policy.

As a partial member of the reservation community, I situate myself within the cultural matrix of fictive kin, friends, and a community that only partially embraced me. Likewise, I propose that the fragments of Fort Berthold women's voices (spoken to me directly or through the distilled rumblings of the "moccasin telegraph"[3]) reflect their own partial truths—as only a fraction of collective assent—about what it means to be Mandan, Hidatsa, or Arikara in the twenty-first century. This question of partiality speaks also to notions of identity, a central theme of the book. Here, narrative fragments are not meant to suggest fractured notions of identity, but rather, a more complex mosaic of kinship, community, ceremonial, political, economic, and personal relationships. I focus on how a particular community of Mandan, Hidatsa, and Arikara women negotiates specific sets of power relations between state structures and community obligations that in turn inform cultural identity. The work histories I elicited from Fort Berthold women help to shape their representations of themselves, as well as mine of them. Anthropologists continue to inscribe their experiences, even as we write culture onto the walls of academe. In these respects, although the assumptions of anthropology may have been effectively dislodged in their reception within emerging multinationalist global economies, the practices of systematically observing, recording, and reconfiguring the daily lives of Others (from Rhode Island factory workers to African griots) remain our disciplinary trademark (Lamphere 1987; Stoller 1996).

Dakota Sioux scholar Elizabeth Cook-Lynn (1996) has asserted that "an examination of the dichotomy between the stories that Indian America tells and the stories that White America tells is crucial to the current literary criticism wars . . . and who gets to tell the stories is a major issue of our time" (p. 64).

Although Cook-Lynn refers primarily to works of literary fiction, her observations speak equally, if not originally, to anthropological representations of American Indians as "vanishing" (cf. Barker and Teaiwa 1994), and the generalized crisis in representation within the discipline of anthropology, flagged by a self-critique and reexamination of the kinds of texts ethnography produces (Marcus and Fischer 1986). In answering the many calls for authorial authenticity, this book situates itself among the considerable critique of anthropology as a colonial discipline, but reasserts and insists on an ethnographic rendering of everyday life as a critical opening to understanding the way that power relations become expressed in the daily tasks and rituals of making a living on a reservation. I therefore do not presume in this context that "writing about" constitutes "speaking for." Rather, by analyzing the effects of state structures on women's everyday lives, I offer only a glimpse into the everyday resistance strategies that inform social life and help to ensure economic and cultural survival.

The Impact of Federal Policy through Time

Although American Indian women's status within domestic political and religious life varies across cultures, in general, American Indian women were respected in complementary gender roles that characterized many Native American societies prior to colonization (Jaimes and Halsey 1992; Leacock 1978; Medicine 1993). Throughout the early reservation period (1890s to 1920s), government policies were aimed at restructuring American Indian life through assaults on Native American religious practices and gender-based relations of production. The overall trend in American Indian policy has been to isolate and then to assimilate American Indians (Deloria and Lytle 1984; Pommershein 1995; Wilkins 1997), first by dispossessing them of their lands, and then by converting them to a variety of Christian religions that reinforced the values of the colonizers. Despite these attempts at Fort Berthold, as in many other reservation communities, women's roles remained centered around kinship relations, in spite of the break-up of the land base into private holdings and the reorganization of consensus-oriented governance into federally chartered government bodies (Biolsi 1993). As a result of U.S. policy changes, women's public status in matrilineal societies, such as among the Mandans, Hidatsas, and Arikaras, declined in direct relationship to the selection of male leaders by U.S. agents and the increase in wage labor, particularly

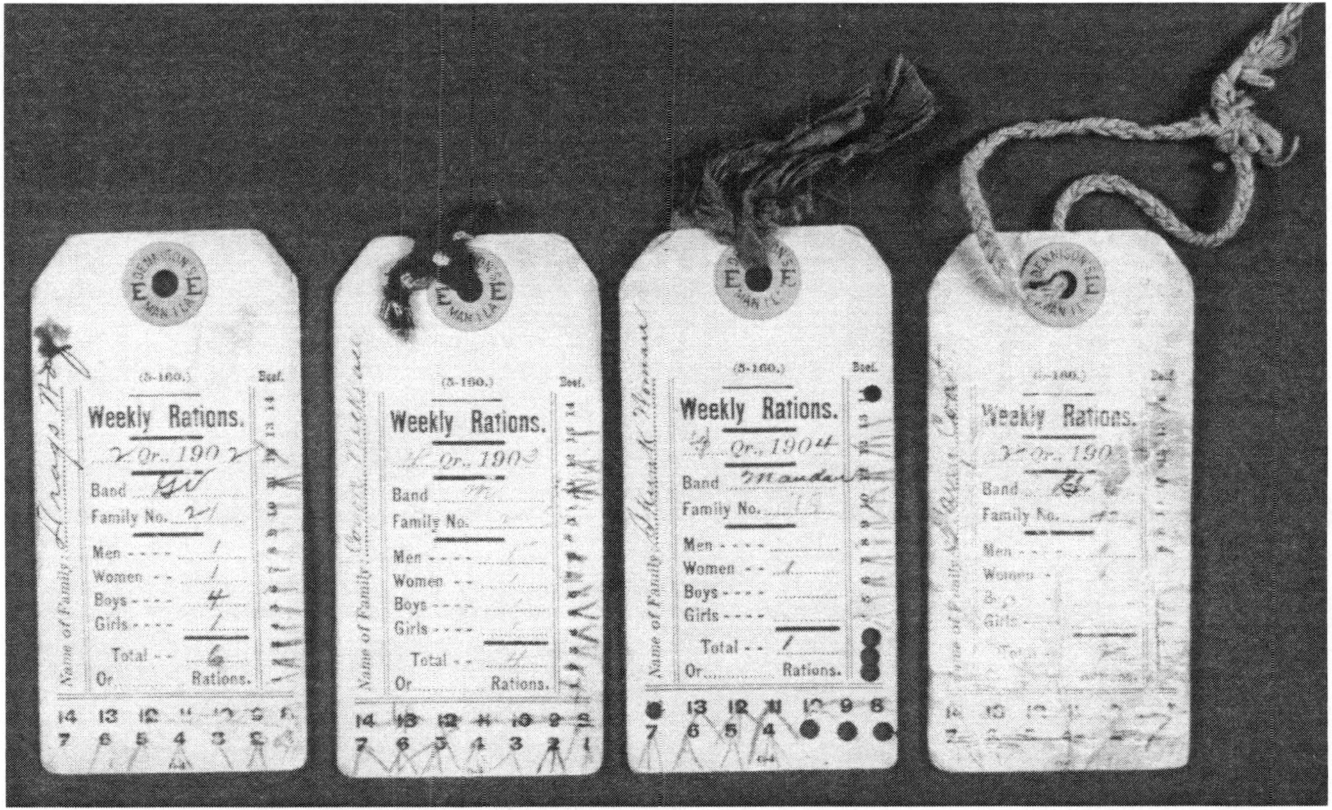

Figure 1.1. Ration Tickets (Dancing Bull), 1902.

for men. Loss of traditional sources of livelihood, in which women's roles were equal to men's, were not compensated. These structural changes in social organization, fostered by early-twentieth-century Victorian family norms of the nuclear family, further eroded women's collective status and security. This was especially true for Mandans and Hidatsas, among whom missionaries and government officials worked in concert to convert a horticultural people to a ranching economy (cf. McLaughlin 1992), thereby devaluing the work of women who controlled their families' garden plots. However, in the areas in which women maintained control over their subsistence activities or developed new strategies based on modified modes of subsistence, they retained a relatively high status in relation to men.

Extensions of women's collective power bases allow them to fill new roles in contemporary work worlds. For instance, Albers (1983) showed the way the increase in Spirit Lake Sioux women's public leadership roles is consistent with prereservation society, which was never sharply divided by a "public" and "domestic" split (Berman 1989). However, formal policy-making bodies effectively overlooked women's contributions to traditional leadership polities and consequently left them out of formal political decisions. In an attempt to bridge tribal and national politics by instituting constitutional governments, the Indian Reorganization Act of 1934 (IRA) effectively wrote women out of tribal leadership. By accepting the IRA form of government, the Mandan, Hidatsa, and Arikara Nations joined political forces and became constitutionally chartered as the Three Affiliated Tribes. As with most IRA governments, men hold most of the formal positions in tribal politics, with notable exceptions, such as first time tribal Chairwoman Rose Crow Flies High, former tribal Chairwoman Alyce Spotted Bear, and several elected councilwomen in the decades since the IRA. Although the IRA formally recognized the authority of tribal governments, former modes of tribal decision making were often transformed by new constitutional frameworks, but practiced nonetheless in extralegal forums that continue to carry community sanction, such as revised forms of women's sodalities (cf. Powers 1986). Community halls, medicine society meetings, clan gatherings, and powwow committees today remain sites for reinforcing customary rules and practices, despite the colonial legacy that attempted to extirpate traditional ways of life.

The 1950s termination policies took aim at tribal sovereignty by attempting to dismantle political structures that upheld the federal-trust relationship of tribes and the U.S. government, a relationship that continues to signify treaty responsibilities. At Fort Berthold, the termination era was marked by two kinds of relocation: one, the result of the Garrison Dam, the other the result of urban job training programs. As one Hidatsa elder proclaimed, in his view, three things have had the greatest negative impact on his people: the 1762 smallpox epidemic, television, and the Garrison Dam.

At a point of remarkable demographic and economic recovery from disease, social reorganization, and dispossession of Indigenous lands, plans for damming the Missouri River were drawn within reservation boundaries throughout North Dakota and South Dakota, lands that had been protected from encroachment by treaty since the 1800s. The final remapping of Fort Berthold was accomplished through joint "compromise" legislation that birthed the 1947 Pick-Sloan Plan, brainchild of the U.S. Army Corps of Engineers. The final plan to dam the Missouri River, which for centuries had been the life vein of the three tribes, was put to a mock vote of the people. The result of this vote is captured best in a well-known photograph of the signing of the bill. In the photograph sits former Tribal Chairman George Gillette. His hands cover his face, his words express his pain: "The truth is," he remarked, "as everyone knows, our Treaty of Fort Laramie . . . and our constitution are being torn to shreds by this contract" (quoted in Meyer 1977, 217). Billed as an issue of energy development in a postwar development boom, the Garrison Dam (which created Lake Sakakawea) generates most of its hydroelectric power for export, fueling cities as far away as Chicago. It also serves to cool the coal refinery plants along its banks. The imposing refinery operation looks on just miles from the reservation boundary in the coal town of Beulah, where long-abandoned subsidiary housing stands hollow at the edge of this company town. The parent company, North American Coal, is one of the largest coal companies in the world, thus situating the reservation economy squarely within the global economy of energy export.

To accommodate construction of the dam, the Army Corps of Engineers relocated more than 90 percent of the reservation population (Reifel 1952). What once was an artery running through fertile bottomlands is now a holding tank that has resulted in five discrete land segments surrounding the water, which rises and falls like a lost ocean in the middle of the prairie (see Figure 1.3). The compensation to tribal members for the taking of tribal lands remains a contested point of dispute, especially between the Army Corps of Engineers and tribal members, as well as between Indian and non-Indian residents (as I illustrate in chapter 4). Most of the Tribes' total compensation funds were spent within the first governmental disbursement period. The Three Affiliated Tribes contested initial monetary reparations when compared against the real value of land, and since the 1986 Joint Tribal Advisory Committee investigations into just compensation for the tribal taking areas. In

Figure 1.2. The Four Bears Bridge.

1994 former Tribal Chairman Wilbur Wilkinson requested more than $30 million in infrastructural compensation through stipulations in the Equitable Compensation Act (PL 102–575 sec 35). Sara, an Arikara woman whose family lands were part of the taking area, explained:

> There was a settlement . . . all enrolled members [received] . . . after 1951; since then we've had two other ones; the largest one I remember was in about 1980 or '81 . . . about $4,000 to all enrolled members; but the money we got during that time, my folks left it in the Agency, so we could get school supplies.

The effects of the dam on land and livelihood have been well documented elsewhere (Berman 1988; Lawson 1982; Reifel 1952; 1986 JTAC Report), including its impact on federally subsidized ranching (McLaughlin 1993) and housing. The reconfiguration of kinship and community through federal land and housing allotments continues to be the result of policy moves that dislocate tribal members from their tribal lands.

The postdam resettlement of the Fort Berthold population coincided with the national push to remove American Indians from their land base and train them to perform wage work off the reservation. To this end, the American Indian Relocation and Vocational Assistance Act of 1955 provided job training programs in urban areas across the country as part of a wider push to assimilate American Indians into the wage labor force. Thousands of American Indians left their reservation communities for urban areas, some of them for the first time. The narratives of Fort Berthold women mirror this trend, as evidenced by the testimonies of the women with whom I spoke. Among those between the ages of forty and sixty, almost all had participated in some form of urban job training away from the reservation. Both men and women participated in large numbers in the relocation programs, despite the fact that urban job training programs offered no preparation for the unfamiliar and often harsh conditions that migrants met with in places such as Chicago, Oakland, Los Angeles, and Dallas. Jane, a Hidatsa woman who went to California on the relocation program, recalled:

> We were given $90 a month . . . for a space a little bigger than a bathroom. It was all Indians, and [the others] were some of the worst people

Figure 1.3. "A lost ocean in the middle of the prairie."

*you could think of . . . alcoholics and drug addicts . . . in that boarding school.
I ended up getting kicked out of there . . . and went to live with my cousin
in San Francisco. My mom was going to sue them [the Bureau of Indian Af-
fairs]. She wanted them to pay for me to come home, but they wouldn't. I
told her, "I'm not a failure; I've got to finish what I started." . . . After that,
I stayed with my cousin.*

Adjustments to new policies often depend on family resources. In particular, the maintenance of kin-based networks—both on and off the reservation—
serves as an important determinant in women's collective action. Whether in
reservation or urban contexts, American Indian women have always drawn on
their kinship networks to resist the alienating effects of government policies.
Furthermore, feminist legal analysts have noted the disconcerting ways that
American Indian policies serve to limit women's adjudicatory power (viz. Mac-
Kinnon 1987). As I discuss at length in chapter 5, some Fort Berthold women I
spoke with on the eve of the Welfare Reform Act of 1996 viewed it as "Termination all over again." *Termination* refers to those policies that attempted to terminate federal-trust responsibilities. In part, this sentiment suggests that welfare
reform, constructed in a political mood of ruthless cuts to subsistence benefits,
delivers a direct blow to American Indian women, who have chiseled a fine line
of survival through a package of benefits outlined by treaties and legally protected by the federal-trust relationship.

The era of self-determination, beginning in the 1960s and continuing into
the present, was ushered in through the reliance on treaties as the precedent and
foundation on which legislative ground was won, especially in land rights and
religious freedom. The inaugural days of the self-determination era drew increasing attention to women's claims, which in turn grew out of land rights and
resource litigation in Indian Country nationwide (Deloria 1985; Stilman 1987).
Landmark legislation of this policy era related to welfare policy included the Indian Child Welfare Act of 1978 (ICWA) (Johnson 1993; Red Horse 1988).

Congress passed the ICWA as a response to social welfare studies that
showed the way child adoption practices over time systematically resulted in the
large-scale removal of American Indian children from Indian homes and away
from their reservation communities. Data from the Spirit Lake Sioux Tribe of
North Dakota (formerly Devil's Lake Sioux) reveal that by 1967, one-third of
reservation children were in out-of-home placement in non-Indian homes (viz.
Hirsh 1991). In many ways, this unwritten policy of removal was an extension of
earlier assimilation policies that established Indian boarding schools at the turn

of the century in an attempt to resocialize Indian children to non-Indian ways (Lomawaima 1994; Archeluta et al. 2000). The effects of these practices reverberate today and find evidence in work histories retold here, especially among elders who remember their first jobs at the hands of government matrons. Carol, whom I introduce here, and whose story I thread throughout these chapters, recalled the predam generation of the early reservation days:

> *I was about eighteen when I worked in a dorm . . . a boarding school for the teenagers, run by the government. They had a dormitory there in Elbowoods. So that the people come from far . . . and this side of the river, they couldn't come across every day so they got them so they could stay in there, stay in that building. My job . . . to begin with I started as a relief matron. Those two white ladies, you know, when one leaves off, they give about four days off, when she gets off then I fill her place. I stayed there and worked clear through, day and night, you might say.*

For decades, the only jobs available to women on the reservation were through government-sponsored agencies, such as boarding schools, the Bureau of Indian Affairs (BIA), and later, the tribal administration. State welfare programs that were instituted in the 1930s later assisted with provisioning household resources, especially in the face of agricultural decline. Where the ICWA was passed to redress more than a century of upheaval and social dislocations, the Social Welfare Reform and Personal Responsibility Act of 1996, by cutting welfare benefits to women and children, was a policy shift that required new safeguards in Indian Country where high unemployment, low mortality, and shifting economic structures (gaming industries notwithstanding) have always indicated that the stakes are higher. Evidence of this runs through federal housing policies, which resituate tribal members in new proximities to land, social services, and each other.

The House of Cards

As the Hidatsa man Good Bird told the anthropologist Gilbert Wilson (1924):

> *An earthlodge was built with a great deal of labor. . . . Certain medicine women were hired to raise [the] posts in place when a lodge was built. . . . The*

four great posts that upheld the roof each had a buffalo calfskin or a piece of
bright-colored calico bound about it to the height of a man's head. These were
offerings to the house spirit. We Hidatsas believed that an earthlodge was
alive, and that the lodge's spirit or soul, dwelt in the four posts. (p. 13–14)

Good Bird's words reflect several concepts embedded in Hidatsa social organization, which matrilineal Mandans and Arikaras share. For example, that earthlodges of the nineteenth century were "built with a great deal of labor" reflects the fact that community effort, as well as seasonal planning, was required for construction of a new house. Women who held the ceremonial rights and knowledge required to build a house were central to its site selection and construction. Where contemporary housing communities are planned outside of collective concern for ceremony and community, Fort Berthold women's kin networks provide a buffer to the fracturing effects of a fragmented land base and a mechanism for reconfiguring community.

To understand how women's networks reshape family and community in housing developments, the way in which land was divided at the initial stages of dispossession (and continues to be subdivided since the damming of the Missouri River) provides a necessary context for analyzing kinship arrangements. The actual and ideological relationship to land is a subtext that consistently emerges in everyday discourse and in specific claims to cultural identity and tribal authority, which the land claims case I discuss in chapter 4 shows.

In my analysis of housing communities, I draw inspiration from Sandia scholar Ted Jojola, who as early as 1973 (seven years after the establishment of the Tribal Housing Authority under the U.S. Department of Housing and Urban Development [HUD][4]) analyzed the relationship between HUD housing and Indian perceptions of their environment at Sandia Pueblo (New Mexico) and Northern Cheyenne (Montana) reservations. Rather than documenting the bureaucratic process of HUD's impact on American Indian communities, Jojola sought "an insight into attitudes" and "interpretations voiced about these housing programs." Where Indian subjects of housing policies are "immersed in a complexity of decision-making," they enact decisions that reconstitute their ethnic and tribal identities in relation to changing community structures (viz. Jojola 1973).

Although HUD project communities differentially impact kin groupings, the social tension lies in the push for "the regularity" of the practice of "being Indian" on the one hand, and the compliance with governmental structures on the other. Housing, especially in the context of planned communities,

Figure 1.4. Mandan Earthlodge, Slant Village Site, Mandan, North Dakota.

is the most intimate symbol of household and family organization. What people do to bridge households reflects new ways of reconfiguring community and reinforcing tribal identity, even in the most socially fragmented housing clusters at Fort Berthold, one of which is colloquially called "the Ghetto."

By relating notions of belonging to a particular land base, families re-create a sense of shared identity through both real and imagined community that often transcends geography (Anderson 1991). As both subtext and metaphor, land guides principles of social organization and identity and links these to a set of shared origins related to time (mythohistorical) and place (sacred sites) (Basso 1996). For example, Mandans associate with a community of common origin within the southernmost segment of the reservation, where the Boy Who Fell to Earth encountered the Old Woman Who Never Dies (viz. Bowers 1950), and where to this day the Lone Man shrine marks a sacred place in this cycle of Mandan cosmology.

Household residency does not necessarily reflect these communities of belonging. Instead, they remain tied to shared family, band, and tribal histories, marked by real and remembered ties to a land base of common origin. At Fort Berthold, the contemporary land base is a fragmented reclustering of communities redistributed around the Garrison Dam. Few families have benefited from land consolidations since the postdam restructuring of the 1960s and 1970s. Residents of population centers in the northern and western segments continue to confront poor water conditions and extensions of HUD policies that force the centralization of housing settlements in proximity to administrative agencies, while rendering a new class of reservation residents landless. Internal political corruption aside,[5] HUD policies have resulted in a decrease in productive land use aimed at neutralizing sovereign land rights, coupled with an increase in land-based natural resource exploitation (such as gas and oil) since the 1970s (Ambler 1990).

Contemporary housing issues and social organization relate directly to the effects of relocation on village-level organization around natural resources—namely, water and timber—and the scarcity of these in the postdam environment. Water, in short supply on the arid grasslands, forces many residents to abandon plans for building on their inherited allotments in the country, settling instead on HUD houses in housing clusters closer to town and community services. This collective move creates stress on shared water resources in those housing areas and has resulted in deep social dissatisfaction, especially for men who are unable to run horses, a symbol of status and prestige, on the limited land provided in housing settlements.

Fort Berthold women's narratives echo contradictory themes of belonging and displacement. In the postdam, post-urban relocation resettlement programs, a house is not always a home. Cory, raised by her grandmother and grandmother's brothers on her grandmother's land in a Hidatsa community, has lived away from the reservation most of her adult life. She and her husband and daughter now live in her mother's HUD house in a rural area of the reservation with her mother and her brother's children. She owns land in scattered allotments throughout the reservation. While her elderly mother rested in an easy chair by the television, Cory and I sat in the kitchen and talked against the scattered punctuation of the slamming screen door as children and grandchildren filed in and out.

> *Some of it was my grandmother's and some of it was an uncle's [mother's brother] and some of it was through trading and purchases. The land's not consolidated. . . . It's just gonna sit there. None of it is being leased out now. There are no houses on any of this land; it's all grass range. . . . I decided against putting a house on it. This reservation, it's kind of a rough place—you put a house up somewhere, it's not gonna be there very long.*

Karen, an Arikara woman living in the reservation hub of New Town, maintains 80 acres and recently had a HUD house built in a distant location, in front of her brother's house where another cross-cousin[6] she calls "brother" lives. Her land is situated close to the shoreline, where she claims that the Tribe has begun survey work for a waterway without her permission. Her main concern is to keep the land in Indian hands, adding that "they're eventually trying to terminate us," once again alluding to the breach of federal-trust responsibility over Indian lands.

Lands that were protected by treaty have subsequently been reduced by government land deals and through federally condemned taking areas. Housing needs are critical on a shrinking land base where lack of potable ground water renders many sites unsuitable for housing construction. A 1987 panel discussed the health effects of the high alkaline water that many people have been forced to drink over the years. A woman from the western reservation segment of Mandaree remarked:

> *On the river bottom we had plenty of water to drink, wash and water our livestock. When we were forced to move to the upper plains, wells were*

dug so deep that you could not pump them by hand. . . . When we moved to the prairie, we could no longer eat the chicken eggs . . . they were blood red because of the water! The water was not suitable even for animals.[7]

The housing "shortage" masks the real fact of a decrease in available land for the people, especially on reservations where the land base has been swallowed up by hydroelectric dams. In the 1970s HUD rental housing, constructed nationwide in the climate of a housing "crisis" in Indian Country, served the public agenda of meeting transitional housing needs. The public face of infrastructural accommodation to house "homeless" Indians now appears to have masked a different kind of agenda—one aimed at clustering tribal members closer to bureaucratic services and under the watchful surveillance of government agents. But even in this process of containment, uprooted subjects stand at attention to the details of everyday life.

When Women Stand, They Stand at the Center

One way to understand Fort Berthold women's centrality in the matrix of HUD policies, resettled communities and reconstituted identities, is from their own positions with respect to communities of memory (Halbwachs 1992; Teski and Climo 1995). In this light, while "memory" may have its particular historical moment of origin—such as the smallpox epidemic or the flooding of the Missouri River—it also embodies a genealogical endpoint, where women rally to affirm kinship and community. *Genealogy* in this context does not constitute "pedigree," but rather an agreed on commonality that links individuals within and across patterned geographies. Examples of both "closed" and "open" spaces reflect the patterned ways that Fort Berthold women reconfigure community in HUD housing projects. Closed spaces tend to be homogeneous communities, such as those configured along old-time band affiliations. Open spaces, such as newer HUD communities, reflect the newly configured ways in which women maintain their kin groupings across dispersed households, especially in the mixed Indian and non-Indian center of New Town.

Matrifocal residence in the context of HUD housing communities can be read within the cultural frame of traditional matrilineal family structures. On the other hand, matrifocality as an extension of matrilineal practices distracts from the daily realities that conscript women to keep up with demands for rent,

Figure 1.5. Rental Apartments for the Elderly.

pressures to sell family allotments and move into HUD communities (creating greater dislocations between land and work), while making ends meet across housing communities. Fort Berthold women do this through a variety of mixed economic strategies, combining formal and informal incomes from activities such as beading, sewing, cooking, and assisting with child care and transportation, and the shuffling of welfare-based incomes among household members and extended kin. In these ways, Fort Berthold women's strategies more closely resemble the African American women described by Carol Stack (1975) in the urban "Flats," where women stand at the center of (re)distributive networks, rather than as the cultural matriarchs of popular mythology.

In "open," transitional, and tribally mixed communities, Fort Berthold women forge communities of identity based on common and agreed on points of origin. As an example, I take the women of the Shell Creek community, located southeast of the reservation hub of New Town. Community members are descended from a breakaway Hidatsa band who left the early reservation for more than thirty years until they were forced to return under U.S. Army escort in the 1870s—the final resettlement period of noncompliant dissidents. These Hidatsa returnees settled at Shell Creek at Fort Berthold. Although most of Shell Creek's original residents now live elsewhere on the reservation, they continue to associate among themselves and relate collectively to their Shell Creek community of origin, despite geographic displacement. Shell Creek women and men link themselves through a common chain of cultural remembrances and have successfully reincorporated themselves in wider reservation life by maintaining their ceremonial links to the past. In tribally mixed communities, such as the reservation hub of New Town, members link households more by social action than by proximity. Women's kin networks serve as the vehicle for reconstructing "old time" family arrangements that have continuing, if tenuous, ties to their common land-based community. These ties bridge the imagined community of the past to the actual maintenance of rural allotments that sit on the grasslands as a rolling reminder of the land that gives to people their sense of belonging.

HUD housing communities may not take on the structural organization of prereservation villages, but "Indian ways," as Jojola (1973) reminds us, remain "practiced with great regularity." Situated at the core of these practices we find "communities of belonging" that link tribal members to self-identity through real and remembered pasts that, in turn, inform cultural identity. The practice of kinship solidarity emerges as a locus where identity is tested and sanctified. Where women's kin networks serve as the vehicle for

Figure 1.6. U.S. Department for Housing and Urban Development (HUD) Rental Homes.

identity construction, they also militate against the dislocation and
tion that result from housing policies implemented from the top dow

Voices from Shell Creek

Shell Creek is similar to other (closed) communities of belonging at Fort Berthold, whereby early reservation settlement patterns reflect band and kinship alliances. In the reconfigured community of Shell Creek (i.e., away from the historic land base), tribal identity crosscuts housing communities by mirroring old-time settlement patterns, much as clans crosscut camps in pre-reservation village settlements.

During the early reservation period, a breakaway Hidatsa band resettled in the Shell Creek community, under pressure by the U.S. government and their Hidatsa relatives, who had earlier accepted government settlements of annuities and allotments in exchange for their chosen way of life. They were rewarded for their efforts to assimilate with log houses and additional trappings (e.g., stoves, axes, knives), which they had to buy with their own annuity funds distributed by government agents. Government allotment policies, the results of which are echoed in women's stories of the difficulty of maintaining house and land as one, served as the instrumental means to contain and control centuries of communal horticulture, hunting, and collecting activities. When viewed in this light, state welfare policies become extensions of early government policies.

According to ethnohistorical accounts, the Crow Flies High band broke away from the Fort Berthold Agency in 1870 over friction at the disbursement of government rations through the Indian Agency, then located at Like-A-Fishhook Village. Approximately 140 Mandans and Hidatsas left Fort Berthold Agency, including the Mandan leader Bob Tail Bull, who was "co-chief" with Crow Flies High (Malouf 1963). This breakaway group migrated more than 100 miles north up the Missouri River to Fort Buford and its surrounding area. Over the course of the next thirty years, band members established summer and winter camps in the region and continued to make frequent forays to Fort Berthold to visit relatives and obtain rations for the duration of their stay.

Nancy is an elder Hidatsa speaker, whose speech patterns raise the possibility among linguists of dialect variations among contemporary Hidatsa language speakers (W. Jones, personal communication). Her grandparents, who raised her, had been part of the Fort Buford camp, and she recalled what they told her of those early days. She sat back in her chair, catching a loose spring on the fold of her floral print, early-reservation–style dress, and explained how

> *in those days . . . they just go around camp, around the river, it's not that they just stayed in one place . . . it's just like you going to Rapid [City, South Dakota] and back.*

Mobility between housing "camps" continues to mark Hidatsa social organization, especially where land remains a tangible and negotiated touchstone. The cadence that "someday I'm gonna fix up that place in the country" resounds with harmonious possibility. With respect to the Shell Creek community, even where individual allottees have moved to HUD housing clusters in the administrative hub of the reservation, their main ties lie with other members of the Shell Creek community. These family "clusters," reinforced by women's visiting patterns, form the core of community values and a shared sense of land-based origins and communal history. In 1894, under U.S. Army escort, the Crow Flies High band returned to Fort Berthold, due to a combination of pressure from government officials and the depletion of wild game. Charlene, raised in the Shell Creek community, recounts what her father, a member of the Crow Flies High band, told her of their escort back to Fort Berthold. She turned down the television to accommodate my questions, and indulged me in the history she recited by memory, as if by her own recollection:

> *This happened in 1894 . . . she [her father's mother] carried three children and the others had to walk. . . . My dad was three years old. He always says, "be good to little ones, I was an orphan at three." These [Shell Creek band] . . . they call them "hoskas,"[8] they're poor. . . . the government told them to come back to Elbowoods [the missionary settlement] and the police were after them, Indian police and white . . . and they go on horseback and they bring them just like they're chasing [them] back. When they got to Shell Creek they didn't want to go to Elbowoods, and they said we're gonna stay here [at Shell Creek], we're not gonna go back. And when they have a house, a log house, after that . . . they [will] get some stoves, just like these*

Elbowoods people. [The ones who settled on the reservation first.] That's what they told them.

Once resettled from Fort Buford to the Shell Creek community of Fort Berthold, the government and the Hidatsa relatives pressured the *hoska* band to accept allotments and annuities in exchange for their former way of life. Following the Dawes Allotment Act of 1887, many of these families remained on unallotted lands.[9]

Even after their final resettlement, Shell Creek village residents remained dissidents who adhered to their traditional practices of polygyny longer than other groups who had come under the influence of Christian conversion agents. Parents withheld their children from attending Christian schools and refused to cut their hair to comply with government requirements. Subsequently, the government withheld food rations and ultimately coerced the Shell Creek people into compliance.

Despite the resettlement hardships suffered by their parents and grandparents, Shell Creek elders recall the early reservation days as bucolic compared to the "coming of the waters of the dam." It was a time when "just about everybody had gardens!" as Maude recalled:

> *I would rather live the way we were before. People had gardens, people depended on each other more . . . when we lived down there [at Shell Creek] people had gardens . . . and people would go and visit them and they'd share.*

The following accounts of Shell Creek women show both the struggle of regrouping their lives from memories given to them from their parents, grandparents, and their own lived experiences. At the same time, their testimonies show the tenacity of maintaining a sense of collective identity through a history of changes and upheavals, and the creativity of refiguring identity and community to meet individual and family needs.

Maude

Maude is a big-boned, strong-willed woman who shares a house at the edge of town with her daughter, a grandson, and an occasional relative living off the reservation. Alongside her block shaped house sits a sedentary mobile trailer, where a nephew sometimes lives. Among Maude's cohorts are a group of Shell Creek women, who despite the distances between their housing communities, continue to visit one another regularly. Shell Creek women, known for their ceremonial rights and possession of respected medicines, stand at the center of their kin networks and the larger Hidatsa community. Hidatsas who identify with other communities of origin, particularly younger people in search of cultural knowledge, frequently turn to Shell Creek women for guidance. What was previously a contentious breakaway group regrouped into a wider network of kin through ceremonial knowledge passed on by women. Shell Creek women not only assist one another, but have rein-corporated themselves in wider reservation life by maintaining and transmit-ting their ceremonial links to the past, thus transforming the knowledge base of kin communities reservationwide. In these ways, Shell Creek women's net-works cut across housing communities to reconfigure band and family rela-tions. So, despite her house at the edge of town, Maude is a frequent visitor to the households of childhood associates from Shell Creek. Since she was seven years old, Maude lived in the Shell Creek home of her mother's brother.

> *Everybody in Shell Creek lived only a quarter of a mile or less than that [in] . . . the village. Nobody would drive around. Well, the fortunate ones, they had cars; most of us didn't have any cars; we just walked. We went to anybody's house; they were all close together. We had a church and a hall and another church . . . right down the hill, and a school . . . Shell Creek Day School. We moved in '50 I think. That's when New Town was built. . . . We had to, otherwise we would have drowned! [Laughs] . . . I don't know why that is, you go to a reservation, that's where they build the dams, why is it? We lost a lot of good land down there. I've tried to live up there [at Shell Creek], I don't know how many times. I even bought a house. It's still sitting there, it's just a shell, and I've barely got one house fixed up, and somebody came and ripped me off. They took all the siding and all the insulation I put in there, so I gave up. I never got any help from the government, I mean from the Tribe. So I couldn't stay out there, I had to move into town and rent a house [and leave the land]. And to make it worse, I was in town with my mother, and here one lady came. They were giving out this General Assistance [GA or welfare], and this girl wanted to get that GA and she begged me, "let your sister stay out there to get the money," so I let her stay there.*

Maude maintains 200 acres at Shell Creek. She leases the land to a white farmer for a crop share once a year. Several times she's had her house vandalized while she's been away from the reservation. Maude said she'd still like to fix up her old log house out at Shell Creek. She wants to build a sweatlodge out there in the summer. Maude relays the story about two non-Indian ministers who came out to use the sweatlodge, so she let them go into the sweatlodge on their own. They poured the whole bucket of water on the rocks and ran out in a mad gasp for air. As she reflected with humor on the sweatlodge fire abandoned by the priests, she recalled a fire at Shell Creek that consumed her house. Rescued from the ashes was a 1920s calendar, a symbol she retrieves from a box of memories from those earlier days.

Charlene

Charlene, like most Shell Creek women, now lives in rental housing outside the boundaries of Shell Creek, but maintains an affiliation with the land there as a marker of group identity and community orientation. However, just as in the days of Crow Flies High when Fort Buford *hoskas* retained their kin networks at Fort Berthold, Shell Creek Hidatsas' networks extend into the other segments of the reservation, as well as with Crow Indians from whom they split in the eighteenth century. Charlene is a member of the Prairie Chicken clan, and her father was one of the last of the *moxohani* clan. She was raised in Shell Creek until age eight, when she went away to boarding school in Bismarck. She picks up and resets photos of her children on a folding table covered with a plastic tablecloth. A handsome young Army veteran, one of her sons, looks out from a photo above them on the wall.

> *Mom told me what it would be like, she went to boarding school. . . .*
> *It was more like a military discipline; you see a man marching them [girls]*
> *around like soldiers. I was there 'til eleven and a half years, [then] I came*
> *back to Shell Creek.*

When her grandmother died, Charlene returned to Shell Creek until she met the man who would become her first husband.

> *We'd sit in the car, sit around and talk. He had about eighteen or*
> *nineteen horses, about twenty-two head of cattle. I wanted to live in Shell*

Creek; Mom said it's best if you two . . . make up your minds [to live some-where else]. If you try to cook or do any housework and you don't do it right, your mother-in-law would always be on about it, or if he drinks, and we don't care for that, then we won't get along.

After her marriage, Charlene left Shell Creek and went to the west seg-ment of the reservation to establish her own household with her husband and to help him raise stock.

I keep house and I ride with my husband during round up time. [After her husband died,] we sold all the machinery, loaded up all the cattle and horses. I had thirty-five, the last sale I had. I sold everything and I bought two lots [off the reservation].

Later, Charlene moved back to New Town and sent her four children to school there for the remainder of their schooling. She met a Crow man from Montana and went to live with him in Billings and on the Crow reservation for almost fifteen years. All of this time, she kept land in Shell Creek and around the west-ern segment where she had lived with her first husband. After her second hus-band died, she came back to Fort Berthold and lived at Four Bears Village, the most densely populated HUD rental community on the reservation.

The house had three bedrooms and a full basement. I didn't move out; when I got married, my son came back after the wedding . . . my kids just stayed so I moved in with [her third husband's] house, and that wasn't paid for yet; and then he has to haul water. It's still there. . . . I can't even haul a pail of water; the ones [her sons] that used to haul water for me, they're not even here now. This is a comfortable place though, I like it. . . . I've been here two years . . . it's out of the wind break.

Charlene considers housing one of the most pressing issues on the reser-vation, adding:

I like homes on their own land, [not] where somebody has to come and inspect their homes, see who's living in their homes. They got no privacy. . . .

I've still got land here [on the reservation], and I've never sold a bit of it. . . .
My children might need them, and my grandchildren might need them. I
just get Social Security. That's it. The only thing I get is that senior citizen
per capita. But that goes for toys [for her grandchildren] and things I don't
need. I was getting VA [Veteran's Administration] pension [from her first
husband, . . . then [because she married her second husband] they cut me off.
Then I divorced him, so I get nothing.

A common scenario in HUD housing designed exclusively for the elderly
is one that gives way to overcrowding in single-dwelling apartments that frequently house extended family members, especially children and grandchildren. Charlene herself accommodated visiting relatives one evening by giving
them the run of her apartment, and without telling them where she was going,
she spent the night sleeping in her car. A walk through these rental housing
units feels far removed from the open prairie life of Shell Creek. Four to six at-
tached dwellings swell with the sound of grandchildren, televisions, and the
constant whistle of the wind through drafty hallways. Yet the necessity of
health and welfare benefits requires that elders live close to town services. Still,
Charlene maintained:

> *I don't like [HUD] housing. . . . But I can't live out there [in Shell*
> *Creek]; I've got to stick close to the clinic.*

Vivien

Vivien is from Shell Creek. In her modest house that she had built next to her
son's house, photographs of her parents look back from the early resettlement
camp to remind her of her origins. According to customary practices, her biological parents gave her to a childless Shell Creek couple to raise. Vivien sold
her predam house to the daughter-in-law of a relative from a community near
Shell Creek. The house itself was moved from its first location at Sanish to
New Town to accommodate the dam. Vivien's grown son used to live in the
house, but now he lives in the trailer in back of the house with his girlfriend.
The trailer has no running water. When Vivien found out that the Tribal
Housing Authority bought the house from the woman, Vivien decided she
wanted to buy it back. It still sits on her lot in town, vacant.

Like Maude and Nancy, Vivien was known in the community as someone "raised by those old people" from Shell Creek who were born before the
1860s. Her first language was Hidatsa, and she remains soft-spoken and ill at
ease among white people, with whom she had little contact throughout her
life. I visited Vivien mostly in the company of other women, especially Maude
to whom she was related. I spent many afternoons in her home, learning
women's arts, and especially, the art of listening. Because she was not comfortable with conducting a formal interview, I include no text from our ex-
changes. Her silence, nonetheless, marks her presence, as it did so many
afternoons in the company of other women.

Nancy

Nancy was raised by the grandparents of her biological father, who, like her, is
a descendant of the *Awaxera'wita* clan (Four Clan) at Crow Flies High Village.
She was married and divorced ("Indian style") to a man she still visits who is
also a descendant of the Crow Flies High group. Her "cousin" Maude, whom
she calls "sister," "comes from" other members of the Four Clan division
(*Chik'sa*), the Chicken Clan. Clan affiliations are difficult to reconstruct from
census data because women were sometimes grouped with their husbands by
government record keepers, or given their husband's names, thus skewing the
matrilineal nature of clan affiliation. What remains important here is the degree to which Shell Creek women identify with one another in such a way as
to provide mutual assistance. To this extent, visiting patterns establish degrees
of solidarity.

My visits with Nancy, similar to my visits with Vivien, were usually in
the company of other women who brought me to visit them, or who were already visiting with these women at the time. Both Nancy and Vivien speak
Hidatsa almost exclusively, and are in general, distrustful of non-Indians.
Maude translated from Hidatsa to English on these occasions, editing her
translations for my limited grasp. Occasionally, Nancy would interject parts of
her story in English for my benefit, such as the afternoon we discussed kinship
and clan relations and the origins of the Shell Creek community.

> *My Dad [the one who raised her] died at 85, and the old lady [her mother who raised*
> *her] was 96. They wanted to go visit [to Fort Buford]. Us' hoskas' . . . were the first*
> *families to come back to Shell Creek . . . All the people from Elbowoods.*

We always had rations. They're like commodities, not to be sold. When they got per cap (from the treaties), they took money back . . . They (the Shell Creek people) all had farms . . . the government gave them. Everyone got (120 acres), certain years, then after that, nobody got any.

The families from Shell Creek were distinct in their resistance strategies against U.S. policies, evidenced also in their language dialect, which reflects both their separation from other communities and their initial stand against compulsory education. Through these cultural commitments, Shell Creek women cross-stitch a pattern of ceremonial knowledge that they weave through each other's kin. Thus, for example, when occasions call for the doctoring skills of a medicine woman, other Hidatsas frequently turn to one of the Shell Creek women. In turn, through reciprocal deeds and obligations, this knowledge (a coveted "commodity") is transferred with care to kinswomen, who, through intermarriage or clan affiliation, may now be one, two, or three generations removed from Shell Creek. Where Bob Tail Bull stepped in as a leader in 1864 owing to his ceremonial rights and knowledge,[10] today, one of his descendants, a Shell Creek woman who inherited his rights, prays for the weather for the good of the people, thus affirming the continuing presence and voice of the Shell Creek community.

Chapter 2

Ceremonial Relations
of Production

*"Maggie can't appreciate these quilts!" she said. "She'd probably be backward enough
to put them to everyday use."*

Alice Walker, *Everyday Use*

To make sense of the social relationships required to participate in contemporary ceremonial life, Mandan, Hidatsa, and Arikara women engage in forms of *ceremonial relations of production*. I develop this concept as a way to account for the contradictions American Indian women face in their response to state intervention and commercial exploitation on the one hand and their resistance to hegemonic domination on the other. In either case, the core of cultural life remains intact. The enduring strengths of cultural practices, in turn, allow new identities to emerge.

The introduction of cash economies to community life has forged new ways of dealing with outside intervention. The contradictory effects of capitalism within the reservation economy not only reflect its market penetration, but also result in ceremonial intensification within the spatial webworks of social relations that straddle more than one site. Ceremonial relations of production distribute power by stretching out webs of social relations across space (beyond the localized work site) and through time as a dimension of cultural history (Massey 1994).

Kin relations intertwine with cultural history to inform cultural identity and anchor it in relation to particular places of cultural meaning and historical significance (Ching and Creed 1997). For example, the Lone Man shrine

31

on the southern segment of the Fort Berthold reservation stands as a testament to Mandan cultural persistence and tribal identity. It is a tangible reference to the cycle of creation brought to earth by cosmological bodies, such as Charred Body and the Old Woman Who Never Dies (referenced earlier in Bowers 1950). Likewise, the Old Scouts Cemetery at White Shield on the eastern segment of the reservation marks a significant place in the history of the Arikara. Both "history" and "mythohistory" connect at the point of oral history, which re-creates the importance of specific places. These places serve as social spaces around which knowledge is transmitted. Relations of production cut across these cultural spaces through intermarriage, clan responsibilities, and the overall needs of the community. In this light, relations of production are constructed "beyond the shop floor," that is, beyond a specific site, but with referential knowledge about it.

With respect to women's work, studies of women's activities typically reify the informal economy as peripheral to discussions of U.S. workplaces, (i.e., "private," woman controlled). Instead, I suggest that the informal economic activities of American Indian women intersect with wage labor, while reinforcing kinship networks in both formal and informal sectors of the reservation economy. In general, kin-based communities facilitate the resilience of women-centered kin networks. In moving beyond the shop floor and beyond the distinction of the informal economy as a separate set of relations of production (c.f. Danesh 1999), I consider the *community as worksite*. Rather than a localized place, *site* becomes "a set of social surroundings, social boundaries and patterns of communit[y]" (Garrell 1992) that reinforces cultural identity through the social relations that give work its meanings. Looking at the community as worksite helps us to redefine the workplace and better understand the tension between kinship and market relations that characterize women's work within the reservation economy. The tension between these two sets of relations takes specific forms in reservation contexts, but they are not unique to American Indian communities. The idea of a community as worksite has wide applicability with respect to the informal economy of women, especially poor and working-class women who enlist their social support networks to supplement meager incomes.[1]

At the center of Fort Berthold women's networks stand *focalwomen*, who, unlike political leaders, are not necessarily visible, although their contributions do not go unacknowledged in culturally appropriate contexts. For example, in their central roles as producers and distributors of goods and organizers of community events, some American Indian women emerge through community consensus as central to community relations. In these community contexts, Fort Berthold women draw on their "invisible skills" as cooks, seamstresses, and beadworkers to organize the community feasts, honorings, and giveaways that lie at the heart of seasonal events. Moreover, *focalwomen* are recognized through public honorings or gift-giving occasions for their ceremonial and kinship knowledge that guides social activities and protocol. The relative positioning of *focalwomen* may shift, depending on the social context, but their knowledge and skills frequently draw them into reservationwide events and issues where they are "called upon" to help out kin and community. In these ways, *focalwomen* help to focus other women on organizational tasks.

Because of their respected positions within the community, *focalwomen* (generally elders who by virtue of age-grading accrue social standing) frequently become involved in political issues, such as working for compensation for the taking of tribal lands and other federal legislatation. In contrast to "activists," *focalwomen* are able to mobilize community-based support because of their culture-based skills in language, kinship, and ceremonies (cf. Sacks 1988a).[2] In these ways, *focalwomen* activate their social networks by drawing on the support of a wide pool of kinship relations. Ceremonial activities, such as preparing for a feast or a public giveaway ceremony, form a baseline from which women resist the devaluation of artistic production, such as making quilts or shawls, items that otherwise might exist solely for market consumption. In community contexts, women set their own standards for production and distribution of goods, and build on their kin networks to meet community needs.

The Heart of Community Is Kinship

Clan relations inform ceremonial behavior by structuring participation for individuals in life-cycle events, such as naming ceremonies and funerals. For instance, Mandan and Hidatsa clans belong to one of two extant divisions, which functioned as moieties throughout the early reservation period (Bowers 1950, 1965 [1992]). These are the Three Clan (*Naginawi*) and the Four Clan (*Nagitopa*) divisions.[3] Although Mandan-Hidatsa assimilation allows us to treat the two subdivisions as a unitary system between Mandans and Hidatsas, elder tribal members still distinguish, for example, between being a *Chik'sa* (Hidatsa) or a *Si'pucka nu'mak* (Mandan).[4] Contemporary marriage practices between Three Clan and Four Clan divisions are less strict than former times, but clan exogamy is still practiced and roundly criticized when it is not. Some Arikara elders talk about "clans," which they associate with the Medicine Lodges (Ghost, Deer, Buffalo, Crane and Eagle, Duck, Moon or Owl, Night, Bear, Mother Corn), and "bands," of which there were thirteen in the nineteenth century. Although these dual ways of structuring Arikara social and ceremonial life remain partially intact, most contemporary Arikaras claim association with the "Left Behind" band, one of the few remnant bands of the original thirteen (see Rogers 1990). "Clan" relations among Arikaras, however, do not parallel the clan constructs of Mandan-Hidatsa kinship, which were formerly integrated with age-graded societies. Anthropological jargon, such as the terms "band" and "clan," has found its way into everyday discourse where technical distinctions fall away. However, all three tribes adhere to classificatory ways of reckoning generational kin, although Hidatsas distinguish between mother's sister, who is classified as mother (*ihuush*), and father's sister (*eshawi*), respectively.

In short, many ways exist of being related and of reckoning kin at Fort Berthold. Whereas clan mergers and extinctions have naturally influenced the overall clan structures, new ways of forging clan relations continue to emerge, and many community educators and elders consciously advocate a revival of clan knowledge. To that end, the tribally controlled KMHA radio station and the tribally administered Fort Berthold Community College continue to sponsor education programs on tribal values, at the heart of which is kinship.

Among Mandans, Hidatsas, and Arikaras, kinship is actively constructed to assert shared group identity and cultural history. Thus origin stories related to the thirteen-clan system, such as the story of Charred Body among the Hidatsa, are told as a means of relaying cultural history by establishing ancestral relationships to specific cultural and sacred sites in North Dakota (Berman 1996b,c). Society bundles, as representative objects that embody cultural origins, reinforce group identity and symbolically anchor kinship ties by marking and ceremonially activating ritual relationships. Cultural knowledge associated with these collective rites is carefully monitored and guarded.

According to Mandan oral tradition, the Mandan people originated from the earth as corn itself springs from the ground. This emergence metaphor is deeply rooted in Mandan cosmology and the ceremonial practices that shape Mandan social life. Corn has been the mainstay of Mandan agriculture for thousands of years and remains a vital symbol for creation, renewal, and survival. As the keeper of the seed, the Old Woman Who Never Dies recurs in the cycle of ceremonies that mark seasonal shifts in horticultural preparations and harvests. The complex of stories and rites related to this cosmological figure directs Mandan ritual cycles by prescribing the appropriate action of cultural members. The relationship of "mother corn" to tribal sovereignty arises in contemporary land claims cases where knowledge about associated garden rites and their associated sites continues to be invoked as a means of staking legitimate claims to cultural identity, as I show in chapter 4. The relationship between kinship and land claims also becomes key to understanding the ways that women organize community life.

To understand how ceremonial relations of production are realized in everyday life, the following section offers a composite picture based on actual events involved with ceremonial production: from amassing quantities of food and goods to their (re)distribution at public events. The practice of gathering donations of food and other items (such as blankets, shawls, quilts, and household goods) reaffirms a shared cultural identity—Mandan, Hidatsa, or Arikara—by acting on the implicit rules that govern social behavior in ritualistic contexts. Lizzy's story draws from multiple experiences that overlap, repeat, and reproduce signifiying events. What persists, and what is illustrated, are the various ways that kin come together at critical junctures in the life cycle to assert kin group solidarity by drawing on their own networks of mutual aid.

Lizzy: A Wake and a Funeral

Lizzy died this week. She had been fighting the slow fight against diabetes for a number of years, until finally, she surrendered the battle. About two weeks before she died, she lodged requests with numerous relatives for her favorite foods: dried deer meat, chokecherry pudding, and corn. Only a few women were known in the reservation community to keep dried meat on hand, and so each was presented with the request. The meat was delivered to an adopted daughter by a clan aunt on her father's side. The daughter, in turn, left the meat with an older "sister" (one of Lizzy's age-mates from childhood). The "sister" arranged for her daughter and her affinal[5] sister to drive from the reservation to her off-reservation residence, where Lizzy had been living for more than a decade.

The meal was prepared in her modest trailer, which sat at the far end of a trailer court, on a familiar plot of corn, beans, and squash that Lizzy and her husband tended to each year in their "home away from home." Lizzy and her kinswomen visited by day, and by night she slept deeply and dreamed of the old days. Four days and four nights after she ate her "last meal," Lizzy died in her sleep, maybe dreaming of the Old Woman Who Never Dies, the bringer of corn and life, or maybe sent off by the red-tail hawk that sat vigil at her funeral site before her burial, then finally lifted off into the lamenting sky when the last handful of dirt was scattered on the ground in her name and memory.

Women gathered up their goods—hand-sewn pillows, blankets, and shawls—and immediately after Lizzy's death, began the daily rounds of soliciting donations of goods, time, and skills, especially sewing. Sewing is the literal thread connecting kinship. With the precision of a jeweler, women crafted quilt upon quilt, until a mound of star quilts seemed to reach up to the Seven Sisters who descended from the sky to become the stars themselves. It felt as though everyone who was connected to Lizzy was busy sewing star quilt tops that week. Pam, a relative by marriage, collected the quilt tops and brought them down to an Indian-owned quilting business to be sewn. A daughter prepared corn soup, a traditional Mandan food, for the feed to be held at the wake—a syncretic service of Christian hymns punctuated with Mandan hand drums and the mournful melody of traditional singers.

A clan aunt was selected as senior pallbearer and this honor went to a Low Cap woman, a member of Lizzy's father's clan. Lizzy was a member of the Knife Clan, or Three Clan division. The pallbearer prepared Lizzy for her journey by ceremonially cleansing her and her home with sage and cedar-smoked prayers, which she offered up in her native language, Hidatsa. In preparation for her deeds, the pallbearer called on one of Lizzy's daughters to ask her true name, her Indian name, the one by which the spirits would recognize her.

The daughters collaborated on what Lizzy should wear, deliberating into the night like a gathering of birds. They landed on their final decision by honoring Lizzy's own wish to wear her elk tooth dress: the same deep blue velvet one she wore in a photo on the wall that looked back on her family now looking back on her life. The daughters stayed as if tethered to the phone, to jot down the names of all callers who would later be gifted at the funeral. In addition to the senior pallbearer, an honorary pallbearer and male pallbearers had to be selected from the family. In this case, it was the young men, classificatory grandsons, who carried the coffin and prepared the grave site for interment. A priest was chosen to officiate over services as a formal gesture to the succesful conversion practices of the Catholic Church. In the public face of Christian ceremony, the customary practice of preparing traditional foods persists, such as dried meat and corn balls, and the supplications offered up in prayer to the spirit of the deceased, away from the funeral grounds and the mourners, in private offering to her spirit on the fourth day after death, when the spirit faces west and journeys into the spirit world.

Ceremonial Work

The best way to understand the ongoing ceremonial cycles of exchange, and the social relations required to carry them out, is by firsthand experience. To this end, I participated in numerous life-cycle events of friends and adoptive relatives, including naming ceremonies, weddings, warbonnet dances,[6] wakes, and funerals. My participation as fictive kin drew me not only into the instrumental contours of women's networks, but the affective and emotional ties that reinforce and ensure intimate relationships. Furthermore, the events surrounding Lizzy's death brought me into the line of service and tested the efficacy of my own cultural knowledge and with what tasks I could be trusted.

I traveled from the western segment to the eastern segment of the reservation (a distance of more than 100 miles) along with Carol, one of my aunties, who had been up the entire night before at a service held in Lizzy's home, yet another 100 miles further. As she watched the hay-stacked prairie roll by from the passenger's side of my car, Carol remarked, "it used to be that all services were done in the home. Not in big halls, like now," adding that it is better to do something in the home, otherwise, she cautioned, "these kids will just go off."

Carol's phone and doorbell rang all day long, constantly calling her back to the house. In her care for the past few weeks, her five-year-old grandson and his friends scampered in and out like squirrels darting through crusty leaves. Carol's daughter went across the street where food was being prepared in the kitchen of another "auntie," a woman whom Carol had taken as a sister in their younger days. We awaited a call from a visiting relative, a cross-cousin Carol calls brother, who had just come home from California and already found himself called on to perform the ritual prayers before the funeral.

I followed Carol's instructions and brought donations of blankets and cash. She had baked roughly seventy cupcakes, and Vee, her adoptive sister, supplied the mixes. I took Carol to the grocery store where she spent additional money on cupcake holders and eggs. I bought corn muffin supplies and borrowed two muffin pans from an Arikara "sister," but in the end, sacrificed the dough to the mealy bugs and abandoned my attempt. Vee and her husband made several raisin pies. Sandwiches, cake, and an unending supply of coffee seemed to flow magically as the women circulated among the fifty or more guests who attended the wake. Additional food was reserved for the feed following the funeral the next day, and once again, the family cooked the meal for the guests.

The Tribal Administration sets aside a wake fund for each family to assist with the elaborate expenses incurred for wakes and funerals in what inevitably become community events. The tribal funds, however, fall short of meeting these expenses. To make up the difference, women rely on their relatives and friends to help out with donations of goods and cash. This generalized reciprocal cycle creates a finely knit web of social relations. These "ceremonial relations" form the core of the informal economy and ceremonial work.

Pam, who had lost her *eshawi* (mother's sister) the year before, told me how she and her husband went into debt for the funeral and that they, along with a brother and sister on General Assistance (GA or welfare), were unable to meet all of the expenses. At the last minute, Pam panicked that she would not be able to afford the genuine eagle feather warbonnet required for the senior pallbearer and placed on the coffin as a sign of respect. So, despite her loosely knit connection to a half-sibling of her mother's brother, she went to the home of this ceremonial practitioner and community leader to request his help for the funeral. Without hesitation, he gave her an eagle feather warbonnet for which he refused to accept any payment.

The actions of her relative parallel the actions that define *focalwomen*. Giving reinforces cultural values of generosity and marks the giver as a respected and cooperative community participant. The gifted in turn becomes obligated to the giver. Focalpeople accrue social standing through giving, and eventually they amass quantities of donations: quilts, blankets, cash, and other items bestowed on them in the public giveaways that take place at funerals, powwows, and social gatherings.

Mauss (1923) detailed early on the power of the gift to reinforce social relations in his great precursor to anthropological exchange theory, *The Gift*. Fifty years later, Marshall Sahlins (1972), drawing from Karl Polanyi's (1944) substantive theory of economics, developed the idea of a "generalized reciprocity," which through gift giving serves as an economic leveler. Sahlins's theory of reciprocal exchange was written against the rationalist models of economics that dominated social and economic thought through the 1960s. Although substantive theories tried to account for social relations by insisting that profit does not always function as a prime motivator for human behavior, feminist theorists later revised exchange theory by pointing out the ways that exchange follows the contours of gender relations, and often serves to reinforce gender inequality, especially where men's goods are accorded greater value than women's (Weiner 1992; cf. Hyde 1989). At Fort Berthold, public gifting at giveaways serves as the public display of leveling social relations. Yet in the private collections and stockpiles of goods *focalwomen* hold, the objects of ceremonial life symbolize more than social standing. Increasingly, and especially since the introduction of cash and commercial goods into the informal and ceremonial economies, social stratification seems (not surprisingly) commensurate with capital accumulation. But, as the characteristics that define *focalwomen* attest to, economic wealth is not the only marker of social status.

Ceremonial knowledge, kinship knowledge, and Native language proficiency significantly contribute to social status and cultural expertise. The arts—especially women's handicrafts—symbolize the ways in which families become connected—from the ceremonial knowledge required to produce specific art forms (such as quilled designs), to collective art production (such as star quilting groups), and ultimately to the exchange and distribution of artworks as we saw in the case of a wake and a funeral. Craft production, like kinship itself, affirms cultural meanings and provides a social space to enact social relationships.

Ceremony or Commodity?

In the nineteenth century, polygynous households characterized Hidatsa social organization with sororal polygyny[7] as a predominant form. Kinswomen, by both proxy and necessity, cooperated in everyday household tasks. The archaeological record tells us that apart from hunting, Hidatsa women procured and processed all food resources, collected water, wood, wild plants, herbs, bark, and reeds (Spector 1983; Weist 1983). Women also worked collectively to process animal hides and to build shelters, and they spent a great deal of productive time in their gardens for which they were responsible (Wilson [1917]

1985). Through the persistence of matrilineal clan structures, contemporary Mandan and Hidatsa women strive to retain control over their productive labor. In former times this was largely in relation to their agricultural work (Hanson 1986), but today the proliferation of cash and goods in ceremonial spheres of exchange affords women new opportunites to control and harness their labor. Women of all three tribes crosscut tribal and kin networks through their collective labor, especially that required for producing the range of artistic goods needed for communitywide events.

In the early reservation period (1879–1910), missionaries targeted both men's and women's productive roles (Klein 1980) with limited regard for those tasks that were previously governed by an indigenous division of labor by gender. Church matrons, such as those assigned to the Congregational Mission at Fort Berthold (Case 1977), taught American Indian women to produce handicrafts suited to Victorian tastes—such as lace tablecloths, napkin rings, and quilts (viz. Gilman and Schneider 1987). In the case of the star quilt, Indian women imbued the Christian motif of the Bethlehem Star with their own cultural meanings. For instance, in Native American cosmologies of the northern Plains, the star quilt design derives from the Morning Star image displayed on buffalo hides in former times and has since been transposed to the Bethlehem Star. Additionally, the American Indian Arts and Crafts Board, as part of the New Deal era, initiated a series of craft production workshops to "reteach" beadwork and porcupine quillwork to Plains Indian women (Schneider 1987; Schraeder 1983; Sheffeld 1997).

One dramatic impact of conversion to Christianity was a decline in age-graded societies, which was a direct result of prohibitions and punishments against the practice of Native religions. Despite these assaults on Native American cultural practices, women maintained their powers associated with visions and sanctioned by women's societies, including those related to quillwork societies (Berman 1998; Bowers 1950). Quillwork, at Fort Berthold and elsewhere on the Plains, is an appliqué art form that carries specific ritual obligations and compensation on the part of the learner to her teacher. In some cases where women dreamed of design motifs, they transferred these ideas to other types of production, such as beadwork and quilting. For example, Plains beadwork closely followed quilling patterns and motifs. Furthermore, where men entered the cash economy through wage labor and agriculture (formerly women's domain), women entered through petty commodity production in the form of arts and crafts. Patricia Albers (1983) has shown for the Spirit Lake Sioux that

Figure 2.1. Kate (Hopkins) Star, Daughter Theresa (with quilt), Early Reservation Period.

although Sioux women were excluded from major annuity and cash-produc-
ing activities . . . *through their own initiative* . . . [they] entered into the cash
economy . . . by way of petty commodity production. . . . [They] manufactured a wide variety of textile commodities suitable for sale or trade in an off-
reservation marketplace. In this manufacture, Sioux women not only used
traditional industrial and decorative skills (e.g., beadwork and quillwork), but
also employed such newly learned techniques as quilting, crocheting, and
lacemaking. (p. 187, emphasis mine)

For Hidatsa women, the relationship between the decline in age-graded
structures and a shift to commodity production parallels a shift to *subsistence*
handicraft production. By the 1930s the reservation economy afforded few
options for wage work for women. However, traditional kin networks and exchange systems continued to function, and through them, women worked to
meet their families' needs by designing the means to supplement government
rations. Although artisan production did not offer women much money, they
at least continued to control production and distribution of their handiwork.

In the current reservation economy, production-for-use and production-
for-exchange have become enmeshed with ceremonial activities so that market
relations and kin-based ceremonial relations have grown interdependent,
forming new ceremonial relations of production. These structural interdependencies between market relations and kin-based relations are a consequence of
the increasing need for cash contributions for ceremonial and life-cycle events.
Wealth differentials likewise require more prosperous families to act on their
redistributive obligations by "giving away" mass quantities of both handmade
objects, such as star quilts and shawls, and store-bought goods, such as blankets
and commercially manufactured cloth. However, within this system of exchange, values influenced by the capitalist economy have resulted in an inflation of the price paid to acquire certain sets of cultural rights and knowledge.
For example, young girls who may want to learn the art of quillwork may not
be able to acquire the necessary forms of payment for ritual induction, even
with their families' assistance. In this way, the market has directly affected the
cost of production by increasing value and demand while skewing the ability of
traditional producers to satisfy that demand. Most women try to generate cash
by working in wage labor when possible or by relying on contributions of cash
and goods from close female kin.

Star quilts, more than any other form of women's arts, figure highly into
both ceremonial and market cycles of exchange. Star quilts confer high status,

Figure 2.2. Quilts Purchased for Public Giveaways.

Figure 2.3. Preparation for Public Giveaway, White Shield Celebration.

both on the giver and the recipient. In contemporary contexts, they are given to mark life passage events, such as births, naming rituals, weddings, and death rites. They also confer honor on recipients for previous deeds for the good of a family or community occasion. In addition, as a traditional marker of identity, star quilts have become emblematic of "Indianness" and the display of generosity. As a result, we continue to see a proliferation in quilt production as a major contribution to social exchange networks. Not only do quilts persist within a ceremonial sphere of production, but also inflation in star quilt giving has raised an expectation in reciprocity that was not previously part of a distributive cycle of exchange. Production-for-sale has changed the nature of social relations that previously governed quilting circles. Women's work groups tend to form along kinship lines, but the inflation in star quilt giving has created greater demand and speed in production. Instead of sewing together by hand, many quilters now work at home on machines. Although this has the effect of privatizing production within the domestic sphere, women still retain control of and are responsible for marketing their own finished products, just as in prereservation times when women controlled the trade of their agricultural products. One effect of capitalism, exemplified by a "putting out" system of production among some quilt makers, is the shift from an interdependent kin-based structure to a hierarchical one among nonrelatives based on supply and demand. However, goods produced for ceremonial occasions or traditional social events (such as dance outfits) are still largely produced through cooperative kin efforts. These art objects assert cultural identity as they move through women's hands along the borders of ceremony and commodity.

Differences in social boundaries created by the needs of the market result in a type of privatization of artistic skills. These skills, nonetheless, are inextricable from the web of social relations that govern the transmission of cultural and artistic knowledge required to produce quality objects. Privatization of production in these artistic spheres has the effect of separating "place" from "space." For instance, in the demand to keep up with the large quantities of quilts required in public ceremonies (such as funerals or honoring ceremonies), some quilt makers work at home, alone. At the other extreme, some enterprising quilt makers have developed entrepreneurial tiers of production, hiring out other women to bat down quilt tops. The community still serves as worksite, but social relations across space create new hierarchies to meet the competing demands of the market and ceremonial life.

The "market" comprises a wide range of outlets that includes museums, galleries, private collectors, regional fairs, and powwows. Goods range from commissioned works to souvenirs for tourist markets, both regional and international in scope. Because Hidatsa and Mandan quillwork remains subject to ceremonial constraints, it has not been incorporated as a market commodity, despite its high value in collector circles. Due to scarcity, recognition of the decline of such items has increased market values. These factors have contributed to marking quillwork as a distinctive "fine art" (Schneider 1980). However, Fort Berthold women resist total assimilation into the market by deciding when to uphold or to bend cultural rules and how to reshape the social relations that govern production and distribution of cultural objects.

Sue: A Quilt for a Bus Ticket

Sue lets the screen door slam after she locks the front door to protect her vacant HUD rental house from vandals. Despite the fact that her rent is only $185 a month, not including utilities, she has been forced to seek temporary shelter with a daughter living off the reservation. She does not receive welfare and receives only a meager revenue from grazing leases on land she holds on another part of the reservation. Her two daughters wait impatiently in the cab of a worn mustard color pick-up truck. One daughter greets me; the other stares on into the distance.

The scenario is familiar to them all. Sue commutes between her daughters' homes, helping them with child care and food contributions. Occasionally, one of her daughters stays behind in the HUD community, when all is well with the house. All was not well with the house the night that Sue came home, turned on the light switch, and stood helplessly in the dark. That day the electricity had been turned off, so she threatened in despair to abandon the house and move permanently off the reservation. This day, she came back to the reservation to pick up her commodity foods because "they were all out of food" at her daughter's house. Sue picked up food from the warehouse distribution center for a household of three[8] to supplement the Aid to Families with Dependent Children (AFDC)[9] that she used to receive for her granddaughter. She searched her house for food and goods to take to her daughter's, and she was glad to have found a package of new sheets in her closet that she used for batting down quilt tops, so now, at least, she could make some quilts and sell them.

A few days later, I accompanied Sue as she made several attempts to sell a star quilt. Sue had to raise $200 in cash for a bus ticket for her son who was stuck in Michigan and needed to get to California. We first went to the house of a friend of mine to try to sell a quilt and pick up some quilt "tops" (the star portion) from my friend. Sue is known as a good quilter. She claims she can make two quilts in one morning. One day when she didn't have a ride out of her house, she made six quilts in one day. My friend said that Sue's quilt tops were "bigger than the one she was saving for," and that "they would be good for donations." I offered to drive her around that morning to try to sell her quilt.

We pulled out of the dirt driveway, kicking up a funnel of dust as we careened onto the blacktop and on to our first stop in a series of visits in an attempt to peddle the quilt. First, we went to Sue's mother's sister's daughter's house. She was not home. Next we went to another relative and, like Sue, a member of the Arikara tribe. Again, no one was home. Feeling a sense of encroaching despair at our failed attempts, Sue suggested we try the local pastor, a non-Indian recently stationed at Fort Berthold from California. His wife, having no need for star quilts because they did not participate in Indian rounds, told us to come back later when the pastor would be home. Finally, we drove to another segment of the reservation to a woman, who, weeks ago, had placed an order with Sue for a quilt, but had never paid for it. Sue figured that this was her chance to make the sale. The woman, known in the community as a hearty bingo fan, arrived bleary-eyed at the door having spent the last closing hours at the casino the night before. Here, after a minor negotiation on the front door step, Sue made her final sale. She drove home relieved that, once again, her son could rely on her for help.

Daily rounds of interhousehold activities, such as Sue's, provide a snapshot of informal work—hustling, trading, provisioning—but it remains only a partial portrait. When women spoke about their work to me in the context of work histories, they frequently called on structural definitions that relate "work" to a wage. Yet, when women described their daily rounds of gathering donations, sewing quilts, preparing for feasts, their sentiments reveal what one tribal member remarked in comparing these tasks to the skills of her foremother: "it's hard work!"

Ceremonial Relations of Production and Hidatsa Quillwork

Hidatsa quillwork is a decorative art form that involves fastening dyed porcupine quills in geometric or floral designs to buckskin objects. The effect is similar to an appliqué (Orchard 1971). Motifs belonged to individual women who dreamed of a particular design. Techniques were learned by a girl from one of her "mothers" or other clan relative (Wilson [1917] 1985).

Prior to colonial subjugation, the Hidatsa were matrilineally clan-based horticulturalists with a complex system of age-graded societies that affected all aspects of social life (Bowers 1965; Bruner 1961). Hidatsa quillwork is intrinsically tied to the ceremonial organization of women's age-graded societies associated with the Woman Above rites (see Bowers 1965). As noted earlier, admission to quilling societies was determined by visions or dreams, particularly those related to the mythical Holy-Woman-Above. Girls who learned how to quill shared visions that entitled them to knowledge of the ritual techniques associated with the technical skills. Failure to comply with proper comportment could result in blindness or other harm.

Women owned rights to production that were passed on ritually through payments (i.e, from a daughter to mother). Reciprocal deeds were also acceptable forms of payment. As Bowers (1965) noted, "A girl would do favors for her 'grandmothers' who had made toys for her or had taught her how to decorate things with beads and quills" (p. 131). In this way rights were preserved within the matrilineage of the clan through a ritualized process of kin-based production.

Quilled goods, although produced by women, had important functions in male ceremonies and village-level political spheres. As decorative arts, quilled items were used in hunting and warring ceremonies and for alliance forming ceremonies, such as the Adoption Pipe (Bowers 1965, 48). Quilled robes and elk-skin dresses, made by a man's female relatives, were given by men to holy women in return for prayers for their hunting exploits (pp. 413–415). In this way, quilling arts were integral to band organization and cooperation, and they functioned both within and between households as items of ceremonial exchange. Women also gained prestige for their quilling skills, and kept records of their accomplishments through "quilling counts." An elder Hidatsa quillworker told me in ranked order all of the quilled items she has produced in her lifetime.

Since the beginning of contact with white traders on the northern Plains, Native American women have produced decorative arts for social, ceremonial, and utilitarian occasions (e.g., from clothing to household dwellings). Mixed economic strategies of the inhabitants of the Upper Missouri included horticulture, hunting, and fishing, whereas the Teton Sioux tribes relied more heavily on hunting and trading for agricultural products with their river valley neighbors. Even though the "old way" of life was disrupted by white encroachment

Figure 2.4. Eagle Woman and Girl Sewing Quillwork.

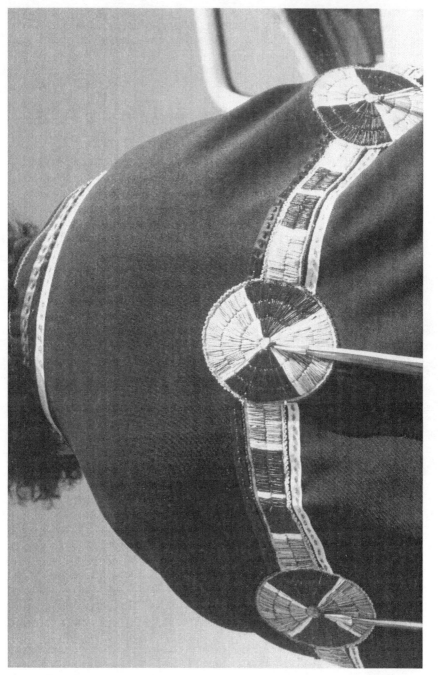

Figure 2.5. Contemporary Hidatsa Quillwork, Woman's Shawl.

and forced resettlement, many Hidatsa women continue to garden, and artistic production in some form or another proliferates within almost every household.

Today, Mandan, Hidatsa, and Arikara women combine a variety of paid jobs, such as working for tribal governments, BIA, Indian Health Service (IHS), or any number of private enterprises that boom and bust within reservation boundaries, with unpaid household labor, including artistic production. Artistic production commonly involves beading and sewing, especially sewing quilts for an unending cycle of ceremonial activities. Despite the constant demand on women's productive labor, most of the work that women do remains in the informal sector of the economy. Lack of jobs in the formal sector is reflected in unemployment statistics for men and women that hover at an average of 75 percent for Fort Berthold and Pine Ridge reservations (BIA, Labor Force Statistics, 1991).

Informal Economy

To subsist in the margins of the reservation economy is to rely on kin and a circulating system of informal exchange. The exchange of objects and services—from sewing star quilts (typically women's work) to shoeing horses (men's work)—serves as a symbolic affirmation of cultural identity reinforced by the kinds of goods and services exchanged (Appadurai 1986). Furthermore, and most important, the relations of production that govern these activities are configured through women-centered kin networks that bridge diverse cultural value orientations. For example, families who identify with rodeos and livestock raising are sometimes critical of Sun Dance-going Indians, but nonetheless, extend their own kinship lines to "traditional" community members, thereby crosscutting dichotomous domains of identity. Women-centered kin networks are constructed across these diverse domains, from funerals to rodeos, that strengthen ways of "being Indian" irrespective of ancestral or linguistic knowledge.

The exchange of goods in informal sectors mirrors commodity distribution flows, described by Taylor (1992) for Rwanda, where differential commodification has an effect on "flows" and "blockages" in circulating systems of exchange. At Fort Berthold, lack of participation and cooperation in the staging of events or projects can be viewed as a type of "blockage" in the system, such as the removal of quillwork from the market. The flow of goods parallels a "flow" of people, such that women act as key distributors of goods across family and community networks, thus carrying goods through these channels of exchange. The exchange of ceremonial goods operates within a closed system, whereby cash can be converted to "art" (such as handcrafted goods), which in turn can be donated for social occasions (e.g., giveaways), then later converted back to cash. Art can also be converted to cash to supplement ceremonial needs or can be used to purchase additional shawls, quilts, blankets, and household goods.

In a market system, the flow of goods is "blocked" by a disjuncture in the system of cyclical exchange, whereby "art" can be converted to cash for disposable cash goods (e.g., a bus ticket). When this happens, value in cultural terms is lost, and disposable cash goods permanently remove energy in the form of human labor from the flow of goods. In short, the circle (of exchange) is broken. The transaction described next further illustrates the point.

The Quilts, Cash, and Pampers Paradigm

A woman with limited means paid a visit to a woman named Jill, who was well-off by community standards, and in her own small network, served as a *focalwoman* for specific ritual occasions. Jill owns her own home and maintains a surplus of blankets and quilts. Midway through coffee, the visiting woman brought out a pair of beaded moccasins that she hoped to sell to her host for $40 so she could purchase disposable diapers and other household goods for her children. In exchange for some cash and a few diapers, Jill was able to add to her stockpile of goods. Recognizing the market value of the moccasins as at least twice the price she was paying (within the reservation), her investment increased her stock, which itself enabled her to serve as an informal pawnbroker.

In this case (see Fig. 2.6) rather than functioning within a system of reciprocal exchange, art is bartered for disposable goods (in this case, disposable diapers) where cash itself mediates the exchange. In this way, cash is generated as needed. In Figure 2.7, cash is also generated this way, but goods are refunneled into ceremonial arenas. For example, from cash generated by the sale of quilts, one family was able to purchase more than $200 worth of food to feed participants of an annual Sun Dance ceremony. Another family converted food stamps to cash to purchase ceremonial goods for the event and raise cash donations for

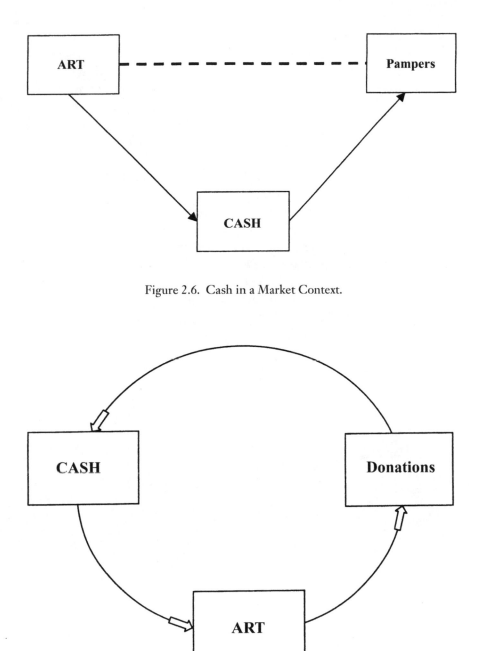

Figure 2.6. Cash in a Market Context.

Figure 2.7. Cash in a Ceremonial Context.

gifts. In this context, the logic of capitalism is challenged: ceremonial goods can be commodified while cash (in the form of money or food stamps) is inserted into ceremonial spheres of activity, thereby lending itself to a form of "commodity fetishism" (Taussig 1980). Ceremonial relations of production intersect both ceremonial and market spheres of exchange, especially when exchange negotiations place equal value on obtaining goods and cash. Most important, it is the *context* of the exchange of goods—market or ceremonial—that determines their value.

Artistic production involves women not only in beading and sewing, but in the marketing of the items produced. Whether women work together or alone in these ventures is likewise determined by the context for the goods. Who are they made for? By whom? For what purpose? Despite the constant demand on women's productive labor, most of the work that women do remains unremunerated. When they work together on artistic projects, from sewing quilts and other items, to their collection and distribution, Fort Berthold women resist the alienating effects of capitalist industry and its privatizing effects on women's work.

Chapter 3

Women, Work, and the State

Plant your garden
Plant your garden
Plant it big and round
then your people
will never go hungry

Hidatsa Corn Planting Song

In a study of Apache and Navajo family values, Bahr and Bahr (1993) asked Apache grandmothers to talk about what they had learned from their own grandmothers. The women answered with stories of work experiences. I take the variety of women's work experiences as my starting point for understanding differences in the way people think about "work" and for uncovering a range of cultural meanings encoded in approaches to work-related activities. Cultural conceptions of work for Apache, Navajo, Mandan, Hidatsa, and Arikara women reflect the importance of work as a process of shared activities, family expeditions, and cooperation (cf. Lamphere 1977). Even wage labor in the formal sector is not unconnected from community and family bonds. The integration of work and family life renders a strictly privatized view of women's work inapplicable to reservation economies. This is not to say, however, that Fort Berthold Indians have not suffered the alienating effects of industry, especially in job training programs that have relocated thousands of reservation residents to urban areas across the country since the 1950s. Yet even in the context of dislocation, tribal members assist one another with job placement and housing needs by creating migration chains that mirror the coping strategies of other rural-urban migrants (Pandit and Davies Withers 1999).

55

Macro structures, such as federal and state food distribution programs, welfare, and employment assistance programs provide a framework against which women's informal activities can be understood as they combine mixed economic strategies to meet the needs of their families and households. Kin-based relations of production extend into formal sectors, where they are frequently (mis)read as nepotism when, for example, tribal employees are criticized for hiring only their relatives. One way of understanding these tensions in the world of tribal hirings and firings is to recognize the structuring principles that underlie job selections as processes that are embedded in the mechanisms of women-centered kin networks. In short, kin networks provide links between family members and opportunities for income. These opportunities range from job placement in reservation-based enterprises, to tribal and BIA employment, and pooling of nonearned income from government-sponsored assistance programs, such as food commodities and food stamps.

Labor statistics vary according to tribal and federal sources, all of which share similar problems of access to household income in the same way that census sources mask data on household size (Lobo 1990/1992).[1] Tribal personnel insist on population undercounts and income overcounts because chronically "unemployed" individuals are not counted in official labor statistics (Beneria and Bisnath 2000; Deere 1991). Nor do labor statistics account for the seasonal and temporary nature of many wage work opportunities, such as temporary work in the gas and oil industries. Together both formal and informal incomes contribute to household economies through crosscutting networks that intersect the worlds of work and community life.

Government Programs that Contribute to Household Economies

Until the 1996 Personal Responsibility and Work Opportunity Reconciliation Act (PL 104–193) was passed, Fort Berthold Indians received a range of government assistance in the form of programs such as Women, Infants, and Children Program (WIC), Food Stamp Program (FSP), GA, AFDC, Commodity Food Programs, and the services provided by IHS and HUD. Most of these programs developed as a result of antipoverty campaigns in the 1930s and 1960s with one major exception in Indian Country: health care, food, and housing are basic living criteria guaranteed to American Indians by treaties in exchange for their lands. Just as the Dakota Treaties referenced in chapter 1 insisted that Indians exchange their lands for a "civilized" way of life, the 1851 Treaty of Fort Laramie, which created the Fort Berthold reservation boundaries, also provided for annuities and food in the form of ration tickets to "settled" Indians. Those who refused to accept the terms of reservationization (viz. Buttes forthcoming) were punished through the "withhold[ing] of the whole or a portion of the annuities,"[2] or fled, as did the *hoska* band from Shell Creek (see chap. 1). I stress this point to underscore the complexity of the rural poverty and community initiative that marks treaty Indians in distinct relationship to government agencies and programs.

American Indians live within the most bureaucratized communities in the United States—beginning at birth when an individual receives a tribal enrollment number. In this context of shuffling food, housing, health care, and education among tribal and federal agencies, state-sponsored programs become income options that Fort Berthold women integrate and manage into their household and community activities. The way in which they do this is governed by their specific needs of maintaining their households and "helping out" kin. For example, although commodity program regulations specify that it is illegal to "use someone else's commodity food," "trade or sell commodity food," or receive commodities *and* food stamps, the economic realities of reservation life make compliance with these measures practically unjust. For example, the income limit in 1990 for a family of five was $1,488 per month, combined allowable income. At nearby Rosebud Sioux reservation, the average TANF payment in 2000 was $205 (Biolsi et al. 2001). In a study of the Food Distribution Program on Indian Reservations (FDPIR), the U.S. Department of Agriculture found that "one out of eight participants reported they sometimes or often did not have enough to eat."[3] The FDPIR operates at 224 reservations serving approximately 135,000 people. At Fort Berthold these services combine warehouse and "tailgate" distribution (i.e., from the back of a truck) depending on the facilities of recipient communities.[4] Commodity distribution days often involve enlisting kin to pick up food supplies for the household recipient, especially if she or he is absent, ill, or unable to arrange for transportation to distribution sites. District council members sometimes assist on distribution days to show support for their constituents.

In addition to commodity food programs, mothers whose incomes fall below $12,000 per year are eligible for WIC services for children up to four years old.[5] In 1992, more than 500 WIC clients lived at Fort Berthold,[6] with seven clinics administering WIC services, such as nutritional counseling. Each

Table 3.1. Monthly Income Limits by
Household Size Governing Eligibility for
Commodity Food Programs.

Household Size	Income Limit
1	$695
2	$893
3	$1,092
4	$1,290
5	$1,488
6	$1,687
7	$1,885
8	$2,083

Each additional household member equals an additional $199 (1992 figures).

check (which must be redeemed for specified foods) averages $38 three times a month for each child. Eligibility, which includes on-reservation residency, is based on similar criteria as commodities (see Table 3.1). In keeping with commodity regulations that stipulate commodities cannot be distributed to FSP recipients, one WIC official summarized that "the whole household has to receive the same benefits." In other words, income averages become a way of resource pooling, but only in formal reporting strategies (wages, AFDC, GA [pre PRWORA], Temporary Assistance for Needy Families [TANF], unemployment, Social Security Income (SSI).[7] Informally, extended kin and household members often pool incomes from these diverse sources. Given the fluctuating character of reservation households, fixed-income bracketing and insurance against mixed economic strategies (such as combining food stamps and commodities) become unrealistic and unfair expectations.

System "abuses" in the context of distribution programs can be read as survival strategies that frequently combine economic and cultural incentives. For example, black market commodity trade serves as part of an incorporative exchange system, whereby large quantities of food can be amassed and prepared for ceremonial occasions (such as wakes and funerals) by drawing on "savings accounts" of commodity products, such as flour for fry bread. In the informal exchange networks of everyday life, food has commodity value in both the bureaucratic and economic meanings of the term. Translated in exchange value, gifts of food are received as "payment" for assistance and given away as "surplus value" and as a display of generosity. Refusal of gifts, in these and most any context, is not only insulting, but marks the refuser as a noncooperative (i.e., socially useless) community member. Within my own reciprocal exchange network, I eventually stockpiled my own "savings account" of commodity food given to me by women I had assisted with other favors. *Focalwomen*, especially those whose knowledge in community events is frequently elicited, generally have a reserve supply of commodities on hand for occasions that call on their ability to prepare huge feasts at a moment's notice. When I asked one interviewee what women do that holds the community together, she replied, "Women cook."

Although "cooking" rightly reflects folk wisdom about the main activities of women, "stockpiling" (not food preparation per se) contributes in greater significance to informal exchange systems. In combination, wages, commodities, gifts, and human labor bridge household disparities among kin while maintaining stratification between household economies. In other words, pooling does not necessarily result in a leveling effect among community members; rather, those households that can afford to contribute more to community functions incur the obligations of kin in an ongoing system of delayed reciprocity.

Wage Work

Opportunities for formal wage work are tied to land consolidation programs in the cattle business (McLaughlin 1993), and the development of tribal enterprises, such as Mandaree Electronics's subcontract with Northrop Corporation and the U.S. Department of Defense, the Three Affiliated Tribes Lumber Construction Manufacturing Corporation, construction of a reservation-based dialysis treatment center, fast food and grocery franchise developments, Fort Berthold Community College, a tribal day-care facility, and the Four Bears Casino. Many Fort Berthold women participate in these diversified ventures, working for the Tribe and the BIA largely as administrative and clerical staff, health-care workers, and educators. Some individuals engage in short-term wage work off the reservation, for example, working in Bismarck for the North Dakota State Commission of Indian Affairs or in the off-reservation town of Beulah at the Coal Gasification Plant.

In both tribal and nontribal enterprises, the Tribal Employment Rights Ordinance (TERO) assists individuals with job placement and work-site grievances. National TERO programs are voluntary organizations that assist Tribes and private industry in Indian contracting, compliance with preference in Indian hiring clauses for on-reservation contracts, job service, civil rights, and violations of fair hiring acts. In principle, the Fort Berthold TERO office fields complaints of racism and sexism in the workplace, but people rarely come forward with either charge. Once, a claim was filed against a reservation-based manufacturing plant for racial discrimination, but the charges were eventually dropped. Sexual harassment is even less likely to be brought under official review. Although I did not solicit this information, women reported various instances of sexual harassment in their work history narratives with the most frequent incidents reported by women who worked as flag women on road crews.

Established in 1978, the TERO has no legal authority to enforce discrimination complaints or compliance with federal Indian hiring preference guidelines. However, it encourages participation and partnerships with non-Indian contractors, especially in gas and oil development. The Dakota Gas Plant (DGP) in the nearby off-reservation town of Beulah employed forty-seven tribal members in 1992, six of whom were women. This 1992 figure was about 7 percent of DGP's total workforce of 650 employees. Technically, according to one TERO source, TERO could enforce higher quotas because "they [DGP] get their water from us to run the place." During a visit to the plant site, I inquired about tribal employee ratios, but the Human Resources division would not release any figures. The white woman conducting my site tour said she did not know anything about minority hiring requirements, especially TERO compliance. A lack of understanding about tribal resources, tax structures, and treaty rights fuels antagonism between non-Indian developers and TERO representatives. During a three-day workshop I attended on TERO orientation, one TERO compliance worker reported that a gun was pulled on him in the course of his duties on the reservation. As the workshop facilitator reminded participants: "We're in a struggle for resources, and the resource is land."

In the context of tribal priorities for economic development (such as a cattle relending program, expansion and construction of community facilities), the women I interviewed held numerous jobs over the course of their lives, and continue to combine nonwage activities with their formal employment. In some cases, individual women have worked for the same firm steadily for more than a decade. Others move in and out of the formal wage sector to meet the

Figure 3.2. Off-Reservation Jobs in Border Communities Not Subject to Tribal Employment Rights Ordinance (TERO).

needs of their kin. Women's work experiences are as diverse as opportunities permit. Reflections about formal work participation provide an opening into women's self-conceptions about the value and meaning of work in their lives.

Women's Work

Helen (Arikara), Supervisor

Helen sets a heavy bag of groceries on the kitchen table, relieving herself of the load at end of her eight-hour shift at Northrop Industries. Her little boy runs in from playing with his "cousin" next door, and her second shift of child care and housework begins. For twenty-five years she has felt secure in her position as one of the first Indian women hired at the Northrop assembly plant since it opened in 1970. Helen expresses a great deal of job satisfaction, preferring the stability of nontribal enterprises to the more capricious whims of tribal employment.

> *[When] I applied for the job, I didn't even know what I was applying for. . . . When I first started, I had no knowledge as to what kind of job I was [going to have]. After I was there for awhile we did that dexterity test. We had to stand there and use our hands. It had little pegs . . . there were little boxes, one side had the pegs and you had to move them to the other side. I was in that group of thirteen that first got hired. It was all Indians except for one white girl and a white guy . . . we really went through some big turnovers . . . at that time, some of them was baby-sitting. [So] they couldn't come to work. At that time, I didn't understand the meaning of a schedule, but now I do.*

In 1992 Northrop still employed several hundred workers, both Indian and non-Indian. Although any project receiving federal funds is subject to TERO's guidelines (including preference in Indian hiring), TERO has not been actively involved with the U.S. Department of Defense's subcontract with the Tribe. Although the primary business of Northrop is assembling parts for airplane bombers, few of the Indian women who spoke with me about their work there mentioned this as a stressful aspect of the job.[8] Only one former employee with whom I spoke stated that he quit his job at Northrop because he could not reconcile making parts for planes used as bombers after his experience in the Vietnam War.

Helen, on the other hand, enjoyed her work and took pride in being a small part of national defense, although she and a sister still joke about it:

> We knew they were government contracts . . . [joking with each other]: I tell her, don't ride on a fighter plane that you made the part for, you may not come back! For me, I'm doing my best, if it goes into a plane, I'm putting someone's life at stake; it's for my country. At no time has it ever bothered me working for the Department of Defense. . . . I always follow it [defense spending] in the paper, 'cause if we don't get the money, I might have no job!

In general, Helen does not feel discriminated against in the workplace. Tensions have flared and resumed over the years with only one grievance case officially reported and subsequently dropped. In fact, she takes pride in having non-Indian friends and often participates in social events that these work-based friendship networks generate (cf. Zavella 1987). On social occasions such as home Tupperware and cosmetic parties, I often consulted with Helen and her sisters for the latest elixir of Mary Kay cosmetics or found myself humbly borrowing plastic containers after failing to attend a Tupperware party sponsored by a non-Indian work friend. As for racial tensions in the workplace, Helen recalled:

> Some of them there were saying they weren't getting treated fair there. All my years that I've worked there I've been really treated good. . . . It was a job.

Although Helen and other Indian women may associate with white women in the workplace or at work-related events, in the larger frame of community assistance with job placement and retention, family comes first. Like other women with steady jobs, Helen assists male relatives with job opportunities, recommending them to employers and helping them to stay on the job. Referring to one male relative, she remarked:

> *I went to bat for him, and I know he got a dollar increase [per hour].*
> *He's steady. He hasn't had to take any days off. . . . The men have come to*
> *work, and you would never think they would work at that kind of job. Some*
> *of these guys were oil field workers. . . . Sometimes I'll ask a man to help me,*
> *like if I turn something and I can't get it unturned. There's been some guys*
> *though, they've really been exceptional [but] that was just a job while they*
> *looked for something that would pay them more money. They're still look-*
> *ing for that job.*

In 1992 the Three Affiliated Tribes subcontracted with Northrop to establish a microelectronic assembly facility on the western segment of the reservation. At that time, the subcontracted company employed fewer than fifty workers. By 1996 only a handful of workers were employed at the subsidiary site. A spokesman for Northrop who came to Fort Berthold told those assembled at a community meeting that after closing its California plant, Northrop came to Fort Berthold when other companies chose to go to Mexico. By casting the net of global economics over the reservation economy, Fort Berthold risks the economic insecurity characteristic of other economic margins, where footloose industry exercises tax incentives, takes advantage of depressed wages, and leaves once hopeful and gainfully employed Indians out of work again.

Helen derived great satisfaction from her work at Northrop and came to rely on the structure and income it contributed to her life. She liked being in a position to be "called on" to help out friends and relatives with job placement and job training opportunities. In the context of her Arikara community, she may not be considered a *focalwoman*, but at Northrop she is able to facilitate opportunities for others because of her seniority, and this brings her the respect that is accorded to people who "help out." The prevailing cultural ethos remains intact: it is not what you do for a living, but who you are in relation to your kin and community that confers social standing in cultural terms.

Cynthia (Hidatsa), Educator

Cynthia invites me inside her new HUD home, situated on the far end of a row of newly constructed prefabricated simulated log cabins. As a recently divorced mother of two, she shows the weariness of juggling her job forty miles away with the demands of child care and housework. With a master's degree from a state university, she is well positioned to work for her Tribe. She has been an educator and administrator, as well as being active in the development of the tribal college. Having experienced the hard living required by most

women who have striven to make it in "two worlds," Cynthia offers the benefits of her experiences:

> *Most of the people on this reservation are living a daily existence . . .*
> *people need successes. It's a hassle to go to school. . . . Give people classes where*
> *they're really going to learn about [what matters]. . . . Fort Berthold suf-*
> *fered the most land loss . . . the flood waters were rising in 1951. Flood wa-*
> *ters were rising and construction had begun. What does that tell people?*
> *"You don't matter!" Some of my older sisters impressed upon me certain*
> *things too. They allowed me to do whatever I wanted to do that would make*
> *me happy. "Don't ever let anyone tell you that this is a free ride—your*
> *grandparents paid for this with the land and the treaties!"*

Despite strong family ties, feelings of isolation and loneliness move
through these women-centered communities, especially in newer housing
communities, where tribal members feel displaced from relatives and communities of belonging. Rural life lends itself to a certain degree of isolation—
sometimes sought, other times weighted.

> *I was twenty-seven when I had my first child. Then I became a dedi-*
> *cated and committed homemaker. We had one car and lived way out in the*
> *country.*

Several women like Cynthia—in their thirties, divorced, formally educated—discussed feelings of loneliness and isolation living out in the country
away from their parents or other extended family. Some of the social fragmentation signified by dispersed families and "latchkey" parenting has been
attributed by some Fort Berthold women to a community in recovery. This
theme is echoed most persistently by health-care workers who deal with the
daily effects of drug and alcohol abuse, but it is a shared perception of a
younger generation of educated tribal members who see themselves as a link
in the process to group recovery for the next generation. Cynthia renders the
historical processes from ethnocide to "policide" in the following way:

> *First people had to get settled on the reservation, then they built the*
> *dam. It's taken a couple of generations for people to work through the pain,*
> *the agony. . . . Okay, I'm a woman . . . the domestic violence program gets*

most of its calls from [this segment]. [We] do not have a lot of social functions other than bingo. There's not a lot of single people [except for] single parents. I'm barely getting through school . . . that consciousness-raising . . . I see the college playing a role there.

This "slice in time" you're talking about [ethnography] is not so long from 150 years ago. My great-grandfather was the last one born at Like-A-Fishhook Village. It takes five generations for a family to heal. If you compare that with Indian policy, you can see the parallel. The first policy was genocide. The second was "well you're not going away, so we'll make farmers out of you" [reservations]. The third was IRA governments [including assimilation policy]. Fourth, relocation [to cities] and fifth, Indian Education and Self-Determination [Act].

The generalized history of American Indian policy is familiar to almost all of its subjects who have endured the generations of social violence and extirpation of cultural practices. As Cynthia poignantly remarks, the failure to kill off, assimilate, remove, and terminate Indian people and their concomitant treaty rights can be measured against the success of Indian people to heal their communities.

One approach to addressing problems of dependency on state distribution is through multipronged programs, which are usually funded at the national level and implemented at several reservation sites nationwide. Fort Berthold, like many other reservation communities, has been the target site for many of these kinds of programs, most of which leave little improvement in overall conditions on the reservation.

Tracy (Hidatsa), Unemployed

Tracy sets down her guitar and brushes her long hair from her shoulder like a mare tossing back a great mane. She makes herself look comfortable in the straight-backed wooden chair across the table from me. She is relaxed and reflective, having taken a year off from work to recover from school board layoffs and to readjust to the silence of single motherhood with grown kids. In the cold of many autumn afternoons, she fed me tea and poetry, and her insights into community development.

[I worked with that] EARN project, Employment Assistance Readiness Net. That was to address the eighteen year old who said, "eh, I'm gonna go

on GA" [and] people on welfare; EARN evolved around this captive group of people. The principle or the goal was to address the dependency that the people have grown used to. The handout . . . to turn that around and enhance the work ethic. The socioeconomic conditions are not conducive to that goal . . . there are no jobs here . . . it was just a Band-Aid. Even Northrop, I don't see them as part of the institution of things here. [So people try it out] they don't show up, or if they work a week and then say forget it.

The college had a subcontract with the Tribe. They hired two psychologists from Minot [University] to come in and interview people. From there they were recommended to go to counseling. We set up the schooling part on adult employability. These people were totally resistant because the system was batting them around again.

One of the largest disagreements I faced everyday was people themselves. . . . They were withdrawn, they were dealing with the manipulation, the oppression. No way could I introduce new thought. They were caught in the system; they were told what to do. . . . They had no choice. They [project personnel] even threatened if this person did not go to counseling, did not go to class, they were going to take their checks away. It was so degrading. They didn't give any real thought to AFDC to young mothers. I'm glad it failed.

Some of the issues raised by Tracy's experience with job training projects conceived by outside agencies relate to common experiences of participants in programs that seek to bring welfare recipients into wage work, but fail to analyze the structures of joblessness and cultural appropriateness of job training programs. The EARN project, billed in part as an economic development project, employed both tribal and nontribal experts to develop multipronged programming. The goals of the program seemed sound on paper—in short, to develop economic self-sufficiency through cottage industries—but the notion of a "captive" target group eliminated choices of self-selection and imposed a system of economic incentive without regard for the *process* of work. For example, as part of the program's goal to develop cottage industries that built on people's extant skills, EARN project personnel attempted to formalize informal economic activities, such as horseshoeing and arts and crafts. As Tracy explained:

[They] highlighted the arts and crafts and totally missed the expression, the art of it. Totally economics, and selling it. [They] were verging on . . . the idea of sale as the fix. The approach was real superficial.

Tracy's critique reflects a common dissatisfaction with programs aimed at enhancing economic opportunities without a full accounting of the social reasons for lack of participation and consequences of failure. Taking Cynthia's and Tracy's accounts together, the effects of federal policies on land and livelihood have been disruptive to the point of despair in some cases. In this context, people are less likely to trust those federal agencies that they have come to associate as the cause of their dependency. When viewed in this light, resistance to state-sponsored programs reads as a form of self-protection against further encroachment on tribal sovereignty and an unwillingness of participants to be agents in the reproduction of their own economic marginality.

Anna (Hidatsa), Secretary

Anna's children fill the lively space of the trailer she and her young husband call home. One toddler cuddles against me while Anna changes another's diaper on the floor. Her eldest girl runs in and out of a slamming screen door and practices her rodeo skills from a bicycle she rides off on against her mother's protests. Anna was raised in a generation where her native language was a lament rattled off the tongues of her grandmothers, but not passed down to her.

> *I say I'm a poor Indian because I never was interested in any of it [Indian history]. . . . My father spoke Hidatsa fluently [but] as far as knowing anything about where we came from, I don't know anything. . . . For us, it was different, it was rodeos.*
>
> *Everything was positive [about living off the reservation]. Sure there's white people with attitude that call us "Indian" and whatnot, but you run into that everywhere. . . . When I moved back here [to the reservation] they were calling me a white kid, and [Indian] kids wanting to fight me.*

Despite her sense of not belonging in the Indian world as a child, Anna's closest childhood associates were her "cousins," or girls she called "sister," and, along with her father's sisters, remain the people with whom she spends the most time. She took her first job, flagging on a road crew, along with her father's sister. They started and ended at the same time. She had three children by the time she was twenty-five and was married in the Assembly of God Church at twenty-six. Her husband works seasonally in a variety of jobs, from construction to truck driving.

He's always been really good as far as that goes. Somehow we've been lucky that he's always had a job. He quit school when he was a junior in high school to work. That February we got our per cap, mine was $10,000 and his was $13,000, and that's when we bought our first trailer and bought a vehicle. . . . [Her husband] worked on oil rigs in the summer, and construction. In between, [he received] unemployment.

On a recipient's eighteenth birthday the Tribe distributes per capita payments as partial compensation for tribal lands. The amount increases with interest, so that current distributions can amount to nearly $20,000.

You just get a check in the mail on your birthday—one lump sum to do what ever you want. In a way, it's no good, because you're only eighteen, and you don't really know yet. . . . I bought a vehicle [and] I bought my dad a horse trailer. I put some in the bank for schooling [and] took a trip to Yellowstone . . . .By the time you're ready to set up house, your money was gone!

Since getting married, Anna has held various jobs working for the Tribe, baby-sitting, and being a full-time mother. Like the majority of women I interviewed about their views on child care and work, Anna distinguished between "baby-sitting" as something she does for pay and taking care of her family's children.

Working at the office, you use your mind, pushing papers. Taking care of kids is physical labor. I baby-sat, but it's hard for me. . . . I don't think I'd be a good child care provider, 'cause I don't have the patience. Or I don't have the bond [with someone else's kids].

Anna fulfills her own child-care needs by relying on her mother's sister's daughter who lives with Anna and her family in exchange for baby-sitting Anna's children. In addition, Anna relies frequently on her mother who often has one or two of Anna's three children in her charge. Despite her feelings about her own abilities as a day-care provider, Anna identifies strongly as a mother and extends her concern for children to the community at large. When I asked what her priority for economic development would be, she responded:

> *It's the children here that need the help. . . . I mean it's not their fault they were born into alcoholic homes. I really feel a burden for these kids who are born into alcoholic homes. . . . Maybe ten years down the line something will be done here—a foster home, instead of breaking up the kids. It just really hurts my heart a lot. . . . I never thought of all these things before. I wonder why they don't have a home here. Or some kind of outreach for these children. And that's something that really gets to me. A social worker [from the reservation] could just not stand how they played politics with these children's lives.*

Other women whose priorities reflected cultural and educational concerns echoed Anna's response to my questions about community development. One of my standard lines of questioning was to ask women: "If you had $1 billion that you could do anything with for community development projects, what would you do?" Several elders (older than age sixty) responded that they would plant gardens, whereas young women, such as Anna, tended to favor child-care and wellness projects.

Corrine (Mandan), Retired

Despite her seventy-five years, Corrine moves about her house with the determination of a small bumblebee in search of nectar. She greets me with a hug and begins to set the table with leftover birthday cake before I have even taken off my coat. Over time, I have variously referred to her as "grandmother," "auntie," and "sister" because we discovered that we were related in multiple ways through adoptive kinship and clan relations. Married to a Sioux man in her younger years, Corrine identifies herself as Mandan, and although she currently lives in HUD housing built for the elderly, she maintains her family allotment in the Mandan community of Twin Buttes.

> *My birthday is June 15, 1917. That's why my daughter keeps having these birthdays. She thinks I'm not gonna be around for the next one! [When I was a girl,] I worked with a lady who was a rancher's daughter. Her father knew my father. She hired me as a cook's helper in an employee's club . . . to feed the people . . . BIA workers. That's where I first worked.*
> *Carol and Diane, my cousins who are always coming here from out west, they were at that school. They'd come in and they'd help me [cleaning pots and pans]. They didn't ask for pay or anything. I'd wash all the dish towels, hang 'em on a line; get everything clean and swept, everything in*

order. Then when everything was in order, then I'd leave. Then my day was over. The next day I'd come right in again at seven.

I didn't finish my schooling. That's the trouble. It was too much for my folks to be taking me and bringing me back. I wanted a job so bad. That [white] lady helped me. They had rooms upstairs . . . for the ones who came from D.C. . . . to check on everything. These rooms all had to be cleaned . . . and that was my job. Some of the employees, they got mad for me. They said I should be getting more money. I just worked myself down. It wasn't even $20 a month, it was less. I couldn't get on as an NYA (National Youth of America) worker, they said I was too old [eighteen]. The NYA was getting $25 a month and I couldn't even get that. They saw how I worked . . . I was the only one [to] wipe, wash, and rinse. Superintendents and principals all came in there to eat—that's when they asked me if I could take that dormitory job. For $150 a month! To me, it was like thousands!

The first place I worked is that Red Buttes school. . . . It must have been about starting in the twenties. . . . The people came from far, like White Shield [the eastern segment of the reservation]. They came across the river; they couldn't come every day, so they built that school there. We had twenty (boys and girls) in each unit. I started as a relief matron. They had four white ladies working here. . . . In between I did clean up jobs. Afterward, I became one of them [matrons]. My "niece" said, "just come and stay with us, and you can go from here." When the other inspectors came in to inspect, they used to say, "Where's your Head [counselor]?" And they said, "There she is!" They thought I was one of them!

I had to go there to see they done it [laundry] right. I trained them too when they cooked. My schooling was all at [Indian boarding] government school in Bismarck and some other outside schools like one house schoolhouses, out where the farmers live. I went to school with the farmers and I stayed with the farmers . . . out in Golden Valley and Dodge. I slept with them in their homes until Friday. Then I'd go back to the reservation. . . . It was too bad weather. So I learned the farmer's ways, how to cook, . . . and so did my brother. And that was good training for us . . . 'cause we were away from our folks.

Prior to boarding school, she recalls a carefree childhood that swung between riding horseback with her brothers and working in domestic service in the homes of white ranchers. Corrine recalls how when she was a young girl at boarding school she was separated from her brother for the first time when they partitioned the boys from the girls. In despair, she ran crying to wrap a clenched fist around the schoolyard fence, and against the pull of the missionary matrons.

> *When I went to Bismarck [to boarding school] I was nine years old. [So] I must have been with those farmers when I was six, seven, and eight. And I rode horseback when I stayed with [her father's relatives]. It was just like moving from one mother and dad to another mother and dad. My youngest uncle and my brother, we all rode horseback . . . but when I was out on the farm and my brother said, "Well, tonight I'm going home, I'm gonna go as far as my uncle's and if he can't take us back, well then we'll just walk on." My brother likes to walk, you know. He'd say, "are you going to come with me or are you going to stay 'til Mom and Dad come after you?" "No, I want to go," and I'd just cry if he was going to leave me. Then I'd follow him. . . . I'd follow him and we'd come back to my uncle's. . . . If they weren't home, we'd just cut across the prairie and just go right home. There were no fences or anything . . . we'd come across herds of wild horses, wild cows, and we had to go around them and go. No stopping too. . . . There were a lot of things I went through with my brother. . . . He really took care of me.*

In addition to suffering the loss of their livelihoods, Corrine's was among the earliest generation to experience the disruptive and punishing effects of boarding school practices. For this generation of elders, work is the most meaningful when it resembles familiar activities of horticulture, livestock production, and hunting.

On a separate occasion, Maude (a Shell Creek elder) and I discussed gardens at length: who still had them and her unsuccessful attempts to keep one in town. Maude remarked:

> *"Now our garden is the Super Value [grocery store] . . . and these commodities."*

Yet innumerable instances of households remain that combine food sources through mixed contributions of household members who continue to hunt *and* shop at the grocery store. Even in the off-reservation neighborhoods of Bismarck, tribal members can be found growing corn and squash on small plots of land in a crowded trailer park or in the middle of a fallow field on the reservation where several women led me to their "secret" plot on the outskirts of town.

What makes work culturally meaningful to elder women is its consistency with the historical and cultural subsistence practices of horticulture. Gardening, as a literal act of cultivation, also serves to reenact those ways of life that persist as symbolic forms of resistance while carving out social relations that reterritorialize space as their own. Not surprisingly, then, when asked in interviews how they would spend $1 billion for community development, elder women repeatedly insisted on the need for community gardens. As matrilineal village societies, Mandan, Hidatsa, and Arikara communities served as viable trade centers on the Plains. Women, who were in charge of their garden plots and its crops of corn, beans, and squash, held central positions in village life and its trading economy. Some elder women maintain neatly plotted gardens, as if in homage to their foremothers. Still others, granddaughters of women who held the knowledge to specific varietal crops, maintain the seeds as both symbol and power of the life-giving force that it holds and in keeping with tribal customary practices to safeguard traditional knowledge.

Elder women transmit values about the need for reconfiguring the old ways into contemporary life to younger women, as evidenced even in young Anna's case. Her $1 billion development project would consist of an in-residency, on-reservation foster home for children so they would not be separated from their extended families and community. Even a "poor Indian" with respect to ceremonial and linguistic knowledge enacts cultural norms in the daily exchange of child-care services through extended family members, and active participation in Indian rodeo events, which, similar to powwows, extend "traditional" activities—from pastoral round-up to public gift-giving ceremonies.

In an informal conversation at the Mandaree community center, I posed my community development question to a member of the community powwow committee. She responded with the local knowledge of one who can see the positive impact of reinforcing cultural values through community-sanctioned projects. "*What they really need here,*" she advised, "*is an arbor for the pow wow grounds.*"

In my zeal to "help out" and affirm the community arbor, I one day found myself hammering nails for its installation with some members of the local powwow committee, all men. I was promptly collected by a group of women who suggested I go with them to buy sandwiches for the men who continued to hammer away at their new project. Not only was this a lesson in what community effort could achieve, but it was perhaps a not-too-subtle lesson in appropriate gender roles and possibly my own transgression. To myself I admitted that I was better skilled at making bologna sandwiches than doing heavy construction anyway.

In the course of recording work histories, I accompanied many women on their daily rounds of visiting relatives, amassing goods, and getting things done. As in my attempt to help Sue sell a star quilt, I participated in numerous ventures to locate markets for women's crafts—both locally and in California. As part of my effort to assist with locating outside markets, I contracted with a California craft cooperative to purchase a specified quantity of beadwork and quilts from Fort Berthold women to market in California. With typical diligence, Corrine sewed steadily until she finished a beaded necklace, for which she received half the amount she needed to purchase a new pair of eyeglasses.

The conversion of sewing arts into cash is nothing new for American Indian women, who were first introduced to the wage sector through craft production in the New Deal era. Following the logic of expansion and contraction of federal funds to welfare-dependent communities, federal block-grant programs in the 1980s and 1990s assisted with state-funneled funds targeted for economic development programs. Similar to the American Indian Arts and Crafts Board efforts in the 1930s, state programs solicited American Indian women's skills as seamstresses, beadworkers, and cooks to bring their informal labor into the formal (wage) sector. By contrast, the 1960s, during which the country at large underwent an expansion of federal assistance, provided opportunities for establishing art-based businesses through direct assistance to Tribes. Following, I contrast the effects of these two eras of federal subsidies on craft production and the policy implications of each.[9]

1960s Co-Op Organization

In the late 1960s, Corrine had just returned from an assembly plant job in California to Fort Berthold, where she quickly found herself at the helm of a new effort to establish a community-based art cooperative on the reservation.

In the mid-1960s, federal funds for community development programs aimed at the underemployed included programs similar to 1930s Job Corps programs, such as organizing arts and crafts for wages. At Fort Berthold, the BIA apportioned seed money to each of the reservation segments by which women could organize cooperative work groups to produce beaded objects for sale. Whereas the BIA representative administered the funds, he did not direct the structure of the work, leaving that instead to community-appointed "leaders" and the self-selection process of the group. The woman who coordinated the efforts of the western segment of the co-op was a key *focalwoman* because of her skill in crafts, education to outside markets, and most significantly, her cultural values and community knowledge, including her involvement with larger political issues (such as her efforts to get compensation for tribal members for the effects of the Garrison Dam). An excellent beadworker and seamstress in her own right (she made moccasins for Presidents Eisenhower and Kennedy), Marie was accorded respect by other women in her community, a critical quality for effective organizing. The BIA-funded beading workshops through which Marie traveled to the various reservation communities to teach the classes. However, it was on the western (Hidatsa) segment, where Marie lived among a wide network of female kin, that the workshops met with the greatest success.

The core members consisted of a loosely structured group of approximately ten women. Membership, as in other informal organizations, tended to fluctuate based on the needs of kin. Marie's sister recalls the initial beadwork classes taught by Marie:

> *The Co-op was run by the Bureau. . . . They had them set up in different segments. [Ours was at] my aunt's house and Marie was the teacher. She taught us how to bead bolo ties . . . we didn't wrap it around, we did it one by one, and that was a lot of work!*

Members of their group included Marie's biological sister, two clan daughters, her husband's sister, two clan aunts who themselves married two brothers, making them sisters-in-law, and the half sister of one of Marie's clan uncles and her sister in turn. Betty, who was married to Marie's son at the time, offered the following description of their work group:

> *After [the BIA] class ended, these nine or ten [women] continued to meet at each other's houses. Whoever's house it was would cook for the rest. They'd each have one type of item to work on that day [e.g., a medallion, moccasins, earrings]. They got a meeting place established and formed their own co-op with help from the Tribe and purchase orders through the state capital that assisted with market outlets. The women each made two items— one for the state, one for themselves. Marie kept track.*

Several points emerge from these women's descriptions that have to do with the structure of the work group and the conditions favorable to its success. First, kinship regulated the selection of the work site, both in the original BIA-sponsored workshops and the later development of an independent cooperative group. In the first case, Marie's "aunt" donated her house for beading classes. Later, women informally rotated houses among the group. Second, relations of production were extensions of women's kinship networks and in this way influenced the self-selection process. As Marie's sister noted:

> *We had real good communication with one another. . . . We really enjoyed it. . . . We'd bring lunch. . . . It united our families.*

In addition, the structure of the initial organization was one of noninterference by the BIA representative, despite his control over the purse strings for the project. The selection of Marie as the project coordinator reinforced the perception that this was an Indian-controlled venture. Furthermore, Marie's leadership qualities were consistent with community values, which made her a respected *focalwoman* to the project. As a community member herself, she understood the intricacies of kinship values, which are the core of Hidatsa culture. These factors combined to propel the women to form an independent co-op that grew out of the kin-based group. The "sell one, keep one" policy affirmed a sense of pride in work that could be sold to outside markets, while at the same time, retained for social and ceremonial distribution. In these ways, the 1960s co-op was *a part of* what went on in the women's daily lives. The co-op reinforced a sense of their identity as Mandan and Hidatsa women.

1990s: The North Dakota Indian Arts Cooperative

In 1986 the North Dakota State Commission on Indian Affairs and the State Economic Development Commission, working at the governor's request, compiled a Native American Arts and Crafts Directory. Under the auspices of the project development specialist, the commission initiated cottage industries, whose base would be the homes of Native American artists throughout North Dakota. One of the explicit goals of the project, from the state's point of view, was to develop opportunities for tourism and trade within North

Dakota to mitigate against the loss of artists to more profitable markets, such as the Southwest. As part of its overall objective, the North Dakota Indian Art Association (NDIAA) was formed "to provide counseling assistance to Indian artists [and] to encourage the development of *art as a business*" (emphasis mine) to all artists on all four of North Dakota's Indian reservations (Standing Rock, Turtle Mountain, Fort Totten, and Fort Berthold).

The project specialist seemed to be a good choice—an artist himself, he was well connected in the Indian art world and an enrolled member of a North Dakota tribe. Unfortunately, one state official, a member of the same tribe, accused him of self-promotion and only "involving his own buddies" in the development of a regional co-op. Gender differences and intratribal tensions were not anticipated as variables that would complicate the collective effort. What was also not foreseen is the extent to which "tribal politics"—that catchall for summarizing internal community disputes—would impede the state's agenda.

When I returned to North Dakota in 1991, the former project administrator had left North Dakota and was making a successful living as an artist in another state. He was replaced by a non-Indian woman with a Ph.D. in a field unrelated to art and with no previous experience working with Native American artists. Highly motivated and well intentioned, the new coordinator was charged with the task of organizing a cooperative that would provide raw materials to artists and an outlet for their goods. Under the umbrella of the state commission, the Great Plains Native American Art and Craft Cooperative emerged as an NDIAA subsidiary, which HUD funded. The North Dakota Micro Marketing Alliance and the NDIAA coordinated outreach projects for the newly formed cooperative. Among these were business workshops taught by instructors from Bismarck State College and craft workshops run by an outreach coordinator who was a skilled artist and an enrolled member of a North Dakota tribe. Policy makers in this case stood outside of the lives of Indian people to configure development programs. Consequently, key factors in how women organize their work experiences and the meanings they bring to their tasks were often overlooked.

Prospective co-op participants were eligible for business training workshops through reservation-based job training programs. To qualify, members had to be eligible for federal GA programs (i.e., their incomes had to be below the poverty threshold of $7,000 per year), and they were required to attend three training workshops. Unlike the 1960s co-op, selective factors were largely economic and requirements more tightly structured with an emphasis on individual achievement. Instruction was by noncommunity members, and business workshops focused on pricing and calculations of an hourly wage. I recall one woman's reaction to the timekeeping process when I visited her at her home. She was worried because she could not find her time sheet, and she was not sure how much time she had invested in making a set of beaded barrettes because her beading activities were constantly interrupted by other household tasks. Her lack of certainty about the accuracy of her timekeeping added stress to her solitary workload.

Significantly, the core group of women who participated in the Fort Berthold workshops were not members of the Three Affiliated Tribes, but had married into the community from other tribes. Despite tribal differences, however, the main source of contention among co-op members was the fact that the project coordinator was a non-Indian with no previous background working with American Indians. Divided ranks between Indian and non-Indian leadership contributed to an overarching lack of focus and a growing perception at the community level that the aims of the co-op were not for the benefit of Indian artists, but an opportunity to use American Indians in public grandstanding for city, state, and national political gains. However, the selection of a regional outlet in a renovated train depot was met with general approval because the depot had originally served as an intertribal trade center, an important symbol of Indian identity in tribal and state history.

By the summer of 1992, renovation of the train depot in the city of Mandan was completed. It opened amidst much fanfare and publicity, including a poster, which lacked any reference to the art co-op that it would house. Some Indians saw this as further evidence that they had been "whitewashed" out of the process. The appointment of an American Indian manager prior to the opening events did little to assuage the skepticism that had been fostered over time. The depot opening was attended by a host of political dignitaries, including the North Dakota State Commissioner of Indian Affairs, the mayor of Mandan, a North Dakota senator and congressman, and a top-ranking official of Burlington Northern Railroad.

Several American Indian artists were invited to exhibit and sell their art and perform musical and artistic demonstrations. "Traditional" Mandan face painting was scheduled, but never took place. I later learned that one of the people who was asked to do the face painting did not have the ceremonial right to do so, and that furthermore, it was not to be done for nonceremonial purposes. Rather than become the subject of community criticism, the artist simply did not show up. Criticism of co-op sponsored art workshops arose on a separate occasion around a quillwork demonstration. At issue was the fact that this art form, at least for Hidatsa women, is associated with strict ceremonial rights and responsibilities incumbent on the learner. In these instances, development strategies overlooked ceremonial rights to production and, in general, attempted to "cut through" extant kinship relations to expedite production of art.

In these examples and others, Indian artists' reaction to essentialist notions of what it means to be "Indian," and in particular, an "Indian artist," took the form of withdrawal from public participation, to outright conflict between Indian and non-Indian organizers. This scenario exemplifies the tendency to exalt American Indian art at the expense of specific cultural practices.

The success or failure of the regional co-op project cannot be measured with respect to its benefits to reservation artists as a whole. The off-reservation depot site continues to provide an income for individual artists on a consignment basis, but many of these artists live off the reservation and in closer proximity to the depot outlet. The goal of some artists remains aimed at wresting control from non-Indian co-op managers. Although the business rationale for developing a regional co-op may be strong on paper, the realities of the North Dakota market (situated within an economic climate of agrarian decline and a history of hostile race relations between Indians and non-Indians) do not lend themselves to a profitable local outlet.

In contrast to the 1960s co-op, the HUD-sponsored project was structured *apart from* daily life. The individualized approach to cottage industry has so far failed to make use of women's extant visiting patterns and family networks and the need to balance art production against other social and ceremonial responsibilities. When cooperative systems are not a grassroots creation, they run the risk of becoming mere arms of state policy and ideology (Canclini 1993; Nash 1993). In broad terms, this is precisely how women's informal economic activities, such as artistic production, become reproduced in the margins by the very programs established to bring them to the center.

Chapter 4

Mihĕ, Mia, Sápat [1]
Women's Ways of Leadership

People can tell just by looking at us what should be done to help us, how we feel, what a "real" Indian is really like. Indian life, as it relates to the real world, is a continuous attempt not to disappoint people who know us. Unfulfilled expectations cause grief and we have already had our share.

Vine Deloria, Jr.
Custer Died for Your Sins

Situated Identities

Identity, like leadership, is not only situated, but becomes expressed situationally and as social relations of power. The expression of multiple identities in the face of reservation-based politics forces a rendering of "difference" that defines American Indian women as Others in relation to outside agencies, organizations, and bureaucracies. Inside the translocalized space of the reservation (Yeager 1996)—that is, a politically moveable and contestable space—leadership qualities of *focalwomen* embody local values of Indigenous knowledge about language, ceremony, tribal histories, and kinship. Outside of the reservation community, public displays of leadership become impossible to disentangle from the politics of location (the reservation) as a location of struggle (hooks 1994).

Why think about place, politics and identity? (Keith and Pile 1993, 34; cf. Ching and Creed 1997). We have seen how women's kin networks act as a mechanism for reshaping place, such as in the ways that Shell Creek women reconfigure community. Likewise, the *community as worksite* spans space, even as it crisscrosses place, to weave an intricate web of social relations (Gupta and Ferguson 1997). In addition, place, as an indicator of mythohistorical linkages to contemporary events, marks space as variously "sacred," "legal," "tribal," and otherwise "off limits" to nonmembers or owners, as I demonstrate later in this chapter in the case of Thunder Bay. Thus, claims to space have critical implications for identity. Local knowledge that tells about where a person comes from ("I am a member of the Waterbuster clan") signifies a set of relational meanings rooted in cultural histories, cosmologies, physical sites, and communities of belonging.

National identities become differentially encoded, especially in site-specific contexts—from Hidatsa women addressing non-Indian employers (a case of a "national" identity asserts itself by a member of an Indian Nation), to national political platforms that reify Indianness in the "expected" ways asserted in the epigraph by Vine Deloria Jr.

We've seen how *focalwomen* stand at the center of kin networks, which in turn regulate the flow of grassroots democracy (cf. Naples 1998). In addition, through their community-based positions, women contribute to the politics of everyday life by reshaping their communities as sites of resistance to hegemonic control (Scott 1990). In electoral politics, they monitor the activities of (mostly male) elected officials in both public and private spheres of activity. As one Arikara woman put it:

> *We know the kind of person they [tribal chairmen] are, after all, we raised them!*

Although institutionalized forms of political leadership provide an overlay to community politics (Champagne 1987, and forthcoming), family networks based in old-time family and tribal affiliations prevail as a parallel political system enmeshed within ceremonial rights and responsibilities. Given this context, many women I interviewed suggest that American Indian women's leadership differs from the public world of political leadership.

Anthropologist Luis Kemnitzer (personal communication), in more than thirty years of research at Pine Ridge reservation, South Dakota, suggests that two forms of leadership exist within reservation politics, "categorical" and "processual." By this he means that some forms of leadership are not formally recognized (categorical), such as "tribal Chair or Chairperson" or "tribal judge," but rather emerge through reciprocal social relations and community consensus (processual). Theresa, a tribal government administrator, likewise asserts that Fort Berthold women have two systems of leadership: political and ceremonial. I take this to correspond roughly to Kemnitzer's categories.

Theresa describes these dual systems as noncompeting, and in fact, through the activities of *focalwomen*, they often overlap. "Traditional" knowledge, as she put it, embodies knowledge about ceremonial arts and the elaborate details required for feasting, honorings, and giveaways. In other matters sit the Tribal Council and Tribal Administration. Attempts to fuse the two systems as one, such as formalizing women's informal activities, are met with resistance and ultimately, failure, as Tracy illustrated for the EARN economic development project (described in chap. 3).

The link between cultural identity and women's leadership can be found at the junction of categorical and processual relationships and leadership qualities. For example, Rose Crow Flies High (Mandan-Hidatsa), a widely respected community leader and first chairwoman of the Three Affiliated Tribes, embodied the qualities most often sought in community leaders. She possessed a strong commitment to her cultural traditions through the use of her indigenous Mandan and Hidatsa languages and was widely sought for her ceremonial knowledge, which remains core to Mandan-Hidatsa values and identity. Her cultural knowledge propelled her into tribal politics, where she led through the respect she had garnered at the community level.

"Madame Chairman" (as she was respectfully called) was strongly influenced by the 1968 Poor People's March on Washington, D.C. She was a key organizer of an American Indian contingent, and in 1992 spoke at the North American Indian Women's Association (NAIWA) conference about this experience. In her NAIWA presentation, she embedded her experience of the Poor People's March in her cultural autobiography with as much salience and historical recall as her references to the 1951 Garrison Dam and the eighteenth-century smallpox epidemic. By bringing her cultural knowledge to bear on key points in Mandan-Hidatsa-Arikara history, Rose Crow Flies High symbolized the convergence of two systems of leadership, which she expressed in the keynote address she delivered to NAIWA:

> *The first thing I have to talk about . . . is . . . our clans on our reservation. . . . This is how we respect one another. I'm a Chicken clan. This Garrison Dam . . . I'm sure you've all heard of how we had to move; this is really sad. . . . Our older people, we lost a lot of them because of moving . . .*

and I still feel bad that we can't have the bottomlands . . . but today, we don't have nothing. I tried to have a garden about five years ago, and I couldn't have one. . . . Sometimes I get lazy and I go [to eat] at the Senior Citizens. [laughs] Many of you must know what it is to be a tribal chairman [sic]: I never had an education; it's my experience that got me there. My parents were poor; and I did whatever had to be done. And it's through experience that I got in on the tribal council. I was the first lady that got on the tribal council and I served six years.

On the subject of leadership, women have a lot to say. They not only influence leadership choices by bringing family pressures to bear and participating in formal election campaigns, but through their kinship positions, they see more incisively into the inadequacies of chartered governments when they attempt to regulate corruption and greed. Some women express disappointment with male qualities of leadership and cite generational lapses in knowledge as contributing to malfeasance. As Martha remarked:

We don't have enough male leaders. Even in the Church. They're looking for power. It's not the old traditional kind of leadership we used to have where you worked for the Tribe. Now it's get as much from the Tribe for themselves and their families. I just don't think there are enough men leaders. There's some coming up now I think. But there's a gap.

Martha also noted two styles of community leadership:

There's kind of two groups: the ones who went on to school and the ones who didn't but have a lot of wisdom from that steady stay-at-home [way of life]. Like Rose [Crow Flies High]. What she didn't know educationwise, she knew from experience. Educators, they have book knowledge, but they don't have the wisdom or the spirituality.

Cynthia, an instructor at the Tribal College, observed:

[A good leader is] someone who hears you, and listens, and lets you know if they can [do something]. Someone who listens and someone who's

Figure 4.1. Former Tribal Chair Rose Crow Flies High Addressing the North American Indian Women's Association (NAIWA) Annual Meeting, Bismarck, North Dakota, 1992.

truthful. . . . The people who get listened to today are the ones with the most clout—[who] can give you the most payoff—to help you meet your daily needs.

Perceptions of elders magnify the gulf between today's political leaders and the council of chiefs in former times, when consensus politics reigned. Maude, who earlier lamented the loss of gardens as a viable source of subsistence, recalled her early reservation experiences and the knowledge her elders imparted along the way.

> *Long time ago, our old men, they weren't afraid to talk to the people. [They used to say,] "You crawl under their bellies," [that's how] they got control of you. You can't even go out hunting now; you have to have licenses!*

Maude's comments reflect both the degree of bureaucratic control tribal governments have over land and livelihood, such as gardening and hunting, and the lack of opportunities for men in traditional modes of subsistence. One Hidatsa man, a Vietnam War veteran, made the connection of men's traditional roles as warriors to serving in the armed forces. During the 1991 Gulf War, enlisted men comprised 2 percent of the tribally enrolled reservation population. Young men lament the lack of opportunities for work on the reservation and the inadequate male role models for boys. As one man told me, "growing up, my role models were the rodeo and the powwow emcees."

Women vary in their views about differences between men and women's leadership. Leadership itself is sometimes a contested idea—where formal organizations struggle to respect collective efforts and anonymity by putting the needs of the group over the needs of the individual. For example, the organizing efforts of a community-based health prevention program operated on principles of collective leadership. Patti, a key organizer of community health programs, stepped outside the spotlight by including all participants in celebration events:

> *[I was asked] who should we call for a photo [for the newspaper]? . . . I said, just announce it [over the P.A. system] "Will the team please gather? You know who you are." They keep trying to give recognition to one person but we won't let them.*

Patti defined a "leader" as one who can cross with ease from formal to informal styles of leadership:

> *People who can get other people to do something. "Tom's" leadership [as a community organizer] emerged just by living there [in his community.] . . . People have tried to organize us, and I just refused. . . . One of these days we'll write a goals and objectives . . . but right now, we're just too busy.*

She characterized women's leadership styles by observing that:

> *Women are not so worried about who gets the credit. They're more concerned about getting the job done—especially with our families. . . . The more people who are included, the stronger the organization.*

And in a twist on the American gender stereotypes that "behind every successful man is a supportive woman," Patti quipped:

> *The men are our backbones because they help us put up the heavy stuff!*

In both public and private worlds of work, women's leadership serves to link these spheres, thus blurring distinctions between the two and raising critical questions about what counts as "work." Women I spoke with frequently characterized leadership as the work that women do. Theresa, for example, described leadership in the following way:

> *Women are called upon to cook. They're behind-the-scenes people who gather those bundles [of goods]. They don't put their names on those quilts or on those shawls. . . . They're doing this for the person who will stand out there in public. And they're cooking up the corn, or drying the corn, or they're at home just maintaining the fire while the rest of the family goes off. There's a lot . . . on the hidden stuff that women do. . . . And then the beadwork that you see, they don't have names on them. I've seen some women who to me are considered "proper" . . . in their own society—not*

*only because they have an education and degree [but] because they played a
role for the generations . . . by keeping the beadwork and quillwork and rituals. To me, that is our leadership.*

In keeping with the qualities that marked Rose Crow Flies High as a respected leader, Theresa emphasized that among the ways that a woman ex-
hibits leadership qualities are by *"keeping that language . . . [and] the dance outfits
for her children."*

Women's qualities are frequently construed in terms of community assistance and the "hidden" world of women's work. Yet, the public display of
food, gifts, and honor given by and bestowed on women in public rituals mark
them as "public" referents who underpin the workings of social and ceremonial life. On the one hand, Fort Berthold women perceive themselves as a conservative force who impart "traditional" values to children through their roles
as mothers. On the other hand, women's everyday work and life experiences
and their continual involvement in ceremonial rounds seem to contradict the
view that women "just maintain the fire." By transmitting extant and transforming kinship knowledge, women reaffirm their group identities as Mandans, Hidatsas, and Arikaras. They also meet political and economic needs of
the community by serving in public leadership roles. How they get to the categorical slot of, for example, "councilwoman," depends on a series of processual choices that reflect community-based knowledge and a strong
recognition of group membership that affirms cultural identity.

Elder Voices: Leading by Example

Martha (Hidatsa-Mandan)

Martha and I sit at her kitchen table where a dance shawl she has been fring-
ing for days lies draped over a chair, giving the impression of a straight-backed
fancy dancer. Her home sits nestled in the prairie where it looks out over
rolling grasses that lead to another relative's house just a short horseback ride
over the hill. She built the house with her own funds on her mother's land
where it sits apart from the uniformity of the surrounding HUD homes.
Martha tours me through her life by way of photographs and newspaper clip-
pings that reveal her family's prominence over time. Martha herself worked

away from the reservation for more than twenty years, but she returned regularly for family and religious gatherings, until she finally returned to her family land for good.

> *Since I've been retired seven years and I came on home, and one thing I've noticed in the last two generations is that the people . . . lost their clanship system and languages and the kinship system. So I've been working . . . and going into homes . . . and whoever would listen to teach our kinship system.*
>
> *I'm Hidatsa, Mandan . . . and we are matrilineal so I am Hidatsa first, Mandan second. The last twenty years I spent in [another state]. I was often the only Native. . . . I always felt all the eyes looking at me . . . in order to survive out there in the white man's world, you always have to be one of the best, 'cause they're there looking at you, and if you make a mistake, [they'll think,] "there's that dumb Indian." So I really felt a responsibility to work at being the best at whatever I did. . . . [There's] no Indian time out there in the white man's world. You're supposed to be there, you better be there fifteen minutes ahead of time. You better be there ready to work!*

Andrea (Hidatsa)

Andrea continues peeling potatoes while her husband, a retired rancher, pulls up on his low-riding jeans and pours us another cup of coffee. Active in both reservation and national politics, Andrea has strong and experienced opinions about what is wrong with the current system of federal subsidies and tribal government.

For many women of her generation, the Kennedy and Johnson administrations spanned years of untiring activism that involved them in campaigns for tribal rights and remunerations for tribal lands and resources, which became banner issues during the Poor Peoples Campaign in 1968. As Rose Crow Flies High emphasized for her generation, American Indian women's participation in the Poor People's March on Washington, D.C., helped to link them to other poor women's concerns across the country. For some, like Andrea, it was a transformative period of social change and introspection.

> *After the Poor People's Campaign, I got involved with the tribal council. We were down there where the poor whites are . . . they're really poor in Kentucky . . . in their shacks. In my time [in tribal government],*

Figure 4.2. National Welfare Rights Organization. 1968 Poor People's March on Washington, D.C. Photo by Bernie Boston©

we created employment for the [tribally run] motor lodge. We hired 125
people. That land belongs to the Army Corps of Engineers so anything they
put underground belongs to the Corps. We had the best . . . then we had
the marina, the gas station . . . the park, picnic tables. Our generation was
the last to know the values of the old way. It was a hard life, but we're used
to it. Now we hand everything over to our children. We even drink with
them! We're destroying our leaders. . . . We'll be sitting along the river
trying to catch fish for a living!

The irony of Andrea's final remark is captured by the fact that fishing
was integral to the "old ways" that she referenced. Like many elders of her
generation and older, the decline of land-based livelihoods marked an irrevo-
cable change in cultural life.

Charlene

Charlene gets up from in front of the television and offers me a can of soda
and a chokecherry ball she made by hand, which she stores in the freezer for
special occasions. I bite into its grainy sweetness, held together with lard,
sugar, dried meat and berries, and shaped like the inside of a woman's palm.
We had been discussing the preparations for a commemorative march that
had involved her parents' relocation from Fort Buford to Fort Berthold in the
late nineteenth century. Knowing that she maintains an active role in public
politics, I asked if she intended to go on the march:

> *No I'm not. I'm going to watch it on TV, if it's on TV, or read about*
> *it in the newspapers. That's something Dad told us to do, stay in the back-*
> *ground. Don't get involved in politics or try to be a leader in some Indian*
> *dance or something. Don't ever do that. I don't. I stay in the background.*
> *I go [to political meetings], but I don't stand up in front and make big*
> *speeches or anything. . . . I don't think there are any good leaders here [on the*
> *reservation]. We're bad. I'll tell you that. There's three different tribes here.*
> *And we never agree on anything. If one comes up, we drag them down. An-*
> *other one tries something, they all laugh and it goes down, you know. It's al-*
> *ways been like that. [Because we're] three different tribes. We don't agree on*
> *nothing. Like the Crow, there's just one tribe. What they do is all in one. They*
> *don't have a bunch of little tiny powwows like we do. They have one. It's called*
> *the Crow Fair, and it's for everybody. That's the way it should be here too.*

Like the community gardens. They had one here by the railroad track. At the end of the railroad track. Right below there we had a 4–H garden for all the 4–H members, but nobody took care of it. And today some of them potatoes will come up and carrots or something will come up. They're wild. And then nobody digs them up. There was one man here that used to come up and dig up all that harvest, whatever he could. He always had a bag and he'd always come down. Like today, he might be shoveling out some potatoes, we don't know!

For Charlene, men were historically in the public role of tribal leadership, and she prefers it that way: leadership based on tribal values.

I would rather have all men [in tribal government]. I would rather have somebody who knows his Indian culture. I don't like these well-educated wise guys. . . . Men have always been leaders of a place, and community events. But you don't want to put a woman there. A woman is more soft-hearted.

Maude (Hidatsa)

I interrupt Maude in the middle of her favorite soap opera, and so together we watch the drama of scorned lovers unfold until the next episode. I reflect on how ethnography, as a slice of life, feels at times like episodic events that find their coherence in the fragments of interpreted lives. Maude and I have spent countless afternoons together, talking about everything from relationships gone haywire to the foibles of tribal politics. The best things, or so I gather from Maude, are the things that are left alone. But nothing, least of all youth, stands still. As she stretches her gnarled knuckles against the cold of the room, Maude thinks reflectively about the question of women's leadership, and who, in her opinion, serves as a role model among women.

You know if I was going to pick someone like that it would be kind of hard. Like this Nancy, she's not educated. But if she was, it would be good. But like I said before, some old people raised her and she's got a lot of knowledge of all the old ways or some of it. And Vivien, she knows a lot. . . . She don't speak such a good English, but she understands it and talks it. Just to come out and use hard words . . . even me, I went as far as eighth grade but when it comes to jaw breakers, I don't know . . . but hers it's not like that, like old ways to have somebody talk or show or teach anybody, I would send them to her. . . .

Like Indian ways, when you get called on to do something, you do the best you can. But now everything is different from way back how it used to be.

We could get those old ladies and talk in a group and go out and teach the kids or either have them come and have a storytelling. Old times and different ones, our ideas, we would tell it. That's what I always do to these kids here. . . . I make them sit down and talk to them. I say, "Don't you say nothing until I get done. Listen" . . . I always talk to them in that way.

Elders display processual forms of leadership that have the potential to be transformed into categorical forms of leadership. In short, they lead by example. This was Rose Crow Flies High's strength, as well as Andrea's and other women who rose to public political prominence through their grassroots community organizing and culture-based knowledge. Even younger women, as in Patti's case, resist individual praise in leadership roles. Models for women's political organization do not mirror white women's organizations (Almquist 1986; Bays 1998; Sacks 1989). Instead, they often resemble extensions of traditional female sodalities that provide the maintenance of tribal ties and the basis for political action. Sometimes, as Maude tells us, the lessons for community lie in the stories told. And who tells those stories remains a critical issue for the transmission of generational knowledge. Without the sanction of elders, "educated wise guys" would carry no clout. It is therefore the elder voices that sometimes whisper like wind on the prairie grass, sometimes admonish like a distant storm, and sometimes register silent resistance to those who refuse to listen.

Ongoing resistance efforts remain tied to land and religious issues. In these arenas, Fort Berthold women combine their ceremonial leadership qualities embedded in traditional knowledge with public political resistance as spokespeople for tribal concerns. Collective and individual organizing efforts are based in a common experience of injustice, especially where community-based issues can potentially unify a factionalized community. The forms that resistance takes vary from nonparticipation in public debates to legal actions against customary transgressions. Women-centered kin networks serve as a mechanism for bridging disputes that may result in fragmented families or communities, as the case of Thunder Bay illustrates.

As early as 1957, the anthropologist Paul Bohannan used case methods to uncover issues that disrupt social life and lead to legal disputes. Textual analysis of Bohannan's testimonies of African Tiv disputes shows that the law itself does not comprise a single discourse (Conley and O'Barr 1990, 5–6). Contemporary critical legal studies extend narrative interpretation of the law and show how claimants do not necessarily represent single identities (Clark 1994; White 1990; Wub-e-ke-niew 1995). Not only is the law interpretive (Sutton 2000), but as the case of Thunder Bay shows, juridical translation occurs at various levels of community where social relations enact social norms.

The Case of Thunder Bay[2]

This case study brings together the relationship between women's kin networks, land, and identity through a land claims case in which women acted on behalf of their families to retain rights to tribal lands. This land claims case involving two families illustrates how identity is contested and reified, and how women's kin networks can bridge community factions.

Methods of dispute resolution parallel structures of leadership and exchange whereby Mandans, Hidatsas, and Arikaras have created two systems of dispute resolution: one that operates within the framework of Euro-American legal principles and constructs, and one that reflects time-honored mechanisms of agreements that reinforce community values of cooperation and consensus.[3] Conflicts in the resolution process may not always get resolved to the satisfaction of contesting parties, but a willingness to adhere to the mediated result, despite the lack of formal enforcement powers, demonstrates both the residents' commitment to community values and the community's power to impose its will through informal means (Lieder 1993, 17). While crosscutting legal and extralegal paths of decision making do not always result in equitable settlements for either or both parties, Lieder's analysis of Navajo dispute resolution also has relevance to Fort Berthold: "When parties are strongly committed to resolving the dispute, the process generally serves to reaffirm group identity by reestablishing harmonious relationships according to community values" (p. 16).

As in other kin-based societies, individuals may not be imbued with adjudicatory powers, but where leadership is necessitated at the level of kinship and community, the common goal of disputants is to reach consensus by trying to resolve matters through family intervention. For instance, among horticultural Hidatsas, clan members in former times were responsibile for enforcing conformity to cultural norms, especially where clanswomen were charged with punishing transgressors of garden etiquette (Wilson 1917). Boundary disputes were resolved through forms of payment, usually in garden products, thus rectifying any appearance of individual accumulation. As

"women's spaces," gardens figure highly in mythological accounts and symbolize the bounty of good work in accordance with proper ritual prescriptions.
But they also serve as sites for disruptive behavior, especially of children and
animals who, as detailed in the exploits of the mythical Boy Who Fell to
Earth,[4] trample women's gardens at their own peril.[5]

Background to the Thunder Bay Case

Idikita'c laid out her field so that it enclosed a small section of road; and she
built a fence around it and tried to keep the villagers from going across her
land. The people did not like this. *Idikita'c* would tie up her fence tight, but
the villagers going down to the chokecherry patch would go right through
her garden, following the road that had been there; sometimes they even
went through with horses. "You must not make your garden here," the people said to *Idikita'c*, "this is a road!" And *Idikita'c* answered, "I do not want
you to do damage to my garden!" There was quite a deal of talk in the village about this matter, and quite a bit of trouble came out of it. (Waheenee
Wea [Buffalo Bird Woman] to Wilson 1917, 110)

The preceding account of nineteenth-century life as told to anthropologist Gilbert Wilson by the Hidatsa woman, Buffalo Bird Woman, shows that
disputes over land date to the early reservation period when family garden
plots served to mark commonly held tracts. Such disputes were generally han-
dled among the families involved and were frequently negotiated among
women who demanded reparations when their fields were invaded. Following
the late-nineteenth-century reservation period when Mandans, Hidatsas, and
Arikaras were forced to relocate from their settlement at Like-a-Fishhook Village up the Missouri River to the Fort Berthold reservation, family disputes
over newly drawn allotment boundaries sometimes erupted in conflict. However, the most contentious boundary disputes continue to involve non-Indian
impingement on Indian land.

Prior to the damming of the Missouri River, Mandan, Hidatsa, and
Arikara women gardened as a primary means of subsistence. The federally imposed allotment system in the late nineteenth century assigned individual men
tracts of land in a matrilineally organized land-based economy. Women accommodated the foreign ideology by naming their gardens after their men-
folk. After the construction of the Garrison Dam, the reservation population

was again relocated. Relocation brought with it new problems of land owner-
ship and distribution—namely, what to do with the shoreline created by the
receding waters of the man-made lake. Although the Thunder Bay case involves tribal members whose primary cultural identification is as Mandans,
the Hidatsas and Arikaras share similar features in their matrilateral decision-
making processes—especially where women act as key negotiators between
family life and tribal politics.

The case of the Thunder Bay road in the Bluff region began with the
formation of the bay as receding flood waters created a newly formed shoreline, marking a new reservation boundary and the end of an old way of life.
Mandans claim that the Thunder Bay case began a "long time ago" when the
Boy Who Fell to Earth made a thunderous landing on his mother's back, and
leaving her for dead, honed his supernatural powers under the tutelage of the
Old Woman Who Never Dies, the timeless resident of Bluff.

> The lodge site was marked by a depression in a plowed field on a terrace
> overlooking the flood plain of the Missouri River. . . . This terrace was the
> traditional site of the home of "Grandmother" or the "Old Woman Who
> Never Dies," a Mandan-Hidatsa supernatural being who insured the fertil-
> ity of crops, especially corn.
>
> In about 1885, the . . . Mandan Corn Priest, Moves Slowly, erected a
> circular earth lodge about 100 yards to the southeast of the depression mark-
> ing the site of the home of the location of Grandmother's Lodge and did not
> plow the terrace upon which it was located. . . . The most prominent land-
> mark close by . . . is said to have been the site of an epic struggle between the
> supernatural, "Grandmother's Boy" and a group of rattlesnakes. Immediately
> below the location of Grandmother's Lodge is the Missouri River floodplain,
> and it was here that Grandmother had her extensive gardens of corn, beans,
> and squash, and that her helpers, the deer, blackbirds, and rodents, assisted
> her in cultivating the soil. (Woolworth 1956).

According to the ethnographer Alfred Bowers (1965), prayers and offerings to
the Old Woman Who Never Dies were as simple as household cleansing rites
and as complex as major bundle transfer rites:

> The simplest and most universal rites were performed by women as individu-
> als or household groups of females and consisted primarily of simple offerings

of meat and pieces of hide placed on sticks in the garden during the northward or southward flights of the water birds. This was often done without benefit of public gatherings or payments to bundle owners. On other occasions a woman, while working in the garden, often dreamed of those spirits associated with the gardens and set up within her garden a high post on which a newly composed personal sacred bundle was hung as a "protector" of the garden. (p. 340)

In the postdam conflicts over land use at Thunder Bay, the importance of the Old Woman Who Never Dies and her adopted son compete with the lure of cash settlements offered to individual allottees by the Thunder Bay Cabin Owners Association. As a particularly important figure for women—teacher of gardening, quillwork, and basketry (see Bowers 1950)—the Old Woman Who Never Dies provides a direct mythohistorical link to land claims by Mandan women of the Thunder Bay and Bluff region. Although the Old Woman Who Never Dies does not overtly enter into the negotiations between the Indigenous residents of Bluff and the cabin owners, Mandan elders invoke the cycle of stories related to her and the Boy Who Fell to Earth as justification for reclaiming the land as a sacred site and as a means of laying claim to their own identity as Mandans.

The Thunder Bay case involves two families, who, like *Idikita'c* and Buffalo Bird Woman before them, own contiguous tracts of land adjoined by a road that passes between them. The original dirt road remains where, before the flood caused by the dam, it provided access to the sites that commemorate the Boy Who Fell to Earth's adventures. This was a private road, maintained by the Indian residents of Bluff. By describing a complex scenario of competing interests for Indian land, we see in the series of events of the case how cultural identity supports claims to legal and political conflict.

Facts of the Case

When the waters created by the dam receded in the 1960s, land that formerly had been underwater remained in the hands of the U.S. Army Corps of Engineers. The Corps passed its own measure to allow the sale of land to individual bidders. The Corps sold the land at public auction in 1962. At the time, the Corps relied on the county, not the Tribe, to gain road easements from reservation landowners, as it had apparently done in the past. Assuming it had the authority to do so, the county built a three-mile road over reservation land all the way to Thunder Bay. As Bluff residents later revealed, the county never had jurisdiction to build a road without permission of the Indian landholders on Indian land.

The Army Corps's land was sold to non-Indians so they could build a resort area for seasonal hunting and fishing. Some sources contend that when tribal members attempted to repurchase shore land, the Army Corps repealed the act allowing them to sell Corps land. By then, the stage had been set for development, and shortly thereafter non-Indians began building temporary vacation cabins along the lakeshore.

By the 1970s, eighteen tracts of Thunder Bay land housed twenty resort cabins, all bordering or surrounded by Indian allotments. To get to their cabins without crossing the lake, the cabin owners had to cut across Indian land on a primitive road never intended for high volume passage, especially for the lumber trucks and speed boats that fueled the cabin owners' drive to build a resort area. In 1976 the county attempted to have the Gray Wolf family's property condemned for a right-of-way, in violation of federal-trust, which stipulates that only a federal agency has the authority to condemn tribal lands.

Not all residents of the Bluff district opposed the right-of-way for the cabin owners. In fact, some tribal members purportedly made land deals with the cabin owners that secured them land in another shoreline district in exchange for Thunder Bay property. Other tribal landowners saw the resort as a potential for economic development and entrepreneurship.

Of the Indian families that lived along the stretch of road itself, the two largest landowners were the Gray Wolfs and the Runs Fasts.[6] Over the course of protests and negotiations that followed, these two families became gridlocked over conditions for granting an easement to the cabin owners along the road. For residents whose family houses remain at Bluff and who have generational ties to the land, the cabin owners' request for an easement reminds them of the steady encroachment of non-Indians onto reservation lands. This reminder reinforces the helplessness that Indians feel over the flooding of sacred sites and fertile bottomlands converted into a playground for non-Indian sport.

In the late 1970s, the Tribe purchased a small tract of land from two Jones women, Mandan sisters whose land was adjacent to the Gray Wolfs' land. The Tribe's strategy has been to buy back as much land as possible, either from individual tribal members, or when possible, non-Indian landholders. The Tribe reasoned that a consolidated land base would allow the Three

Affiliated Tribes to pursue their own economic development plans. The effect is that individual tribal members are increasingly rendered landless, while the Tribal business council negotiates land deals and business contracts with non-Indian investors. One tribal member, John, told me that his brother was looking into starting his own marina boat launch on another segment of the reservation and was told that "the Army Corps . . . would give the go-ahead" on development if they could get an easement passed on Thunder Bay.

John referred to the stall as a case of "blackmail," pitting one tribal member's interests against another's. Ironically, Mrs. Runs Fast's resistance to an easement and John's brother's willingness to develop his part of the shoreline on another part of the reservation become intertwined in ways not readily apparent. In this instance, the Army Corps of Engineers used one family's interests against the others' to levy support for lakeshore development to benefit a non-Indian community: the Thunder Bay cabin owners.

The Indian landowners in Bluff eventually learned that cabin owners had been passing on their road without a right-of-way for more than ten years. The residents along the road petitioned for back payments in trespass damages that the BIA issued annually. In frustration, Lorna Gray Wolf elicited the help of her family and friends to dig a trench across the road. The trench, four feet wide by four feet deep and almost seventy-five feet long, effectively blocked cabin owners from reaching their lakeshore homes. She made three trips from her temporary home off the reservation to oversee the project.

> *We came out with a backhoe . . . [and] put up many signs . . . [but] they [cabin owners] just shot them up.*

The incident, which brought local and statewide publicity to the case, drew attention to the fact that the cabin owners had been trespassing across Indian land since construction of their resort homes first began. They reportedly denied crossing access to Gray Wolf family members who wanted to make ceremonial offerings at sacred sites.

The cabin owners, having yet no legal right-of-way, went around the trench and in the process tore up Gray Wolf land. The cabin owners eventually agreed to back payments for trespass damages, but the Gray Wolf and Runs Fast women claim that these payments do not begin to cover the vandalism damage done to their houses along the road.

Figure 4.3. Shot-up Sign on Indian Land Easement Where a Trench Was Dug to Prevent Passage.

After more than ten years of litigation, bureaucratic harassment, destruction to her property, and threats on her brother's life, Lorna Gray Wolf agreed to sign the easement that grants her roughly $5,000 over twenty-eight years for each eighty-acre tract. Most allotments are shared interest tracts with any revenue derived from oil, gas, grazing, or easements split among all shareholders. For the BIA to approve the easement, it must be signed by all parties.

Mrs. Runs Fast's land and the house she grew up in lie on the other side of the road. Mrs. Runs Fast holds this eighty-acre plot in common with her niece and adopted brother. Therefore, any income must be split three ways. The total amount received for her share of the easement is $198 per year. Considering she was seventy-two years old at the time, Mrs. Runs Fast's daughter argued for a lump-sum settlement. The cabin owners rejected the suggestion, and the tribal attorney's secretary reminded Mrs. Runs Fast that her Social Security benefits (her sole source of income) would be sharply reduced if she received any other income, and the rent for her elderly housing unit would go up in compliance with Fort Berthold Housing Authority's income/rent ratio.

Both BIA representatives and her own district councilman tell Mrs. Runs Fast that she will be "losing out" on money that would go to the Gray Wolfs if she refuses to sign. She receives telephone calls from lawyers representing the newly formed Thunder Bay Cabin Owners Association who pressure her to sign the easement. A congressman calls the BIA superintendent threatening a potential adverse impact on federally funded Indian housing projects if the cabin owners (reputed friends of congressmen and senators) are denied access by the road. The superintendent stresses his responsibility to hold the trust relationship for individual Indians and the Tribe, and tells Mrs. Runs Fast and her family that they will not take action on Indian land for the benefit of non-Indians, but the whole ordeal could end if Mrs. Runs Fast would simply sign the easement. Mrs. Runs Fast refuses to sign. She receives more telephone calls from lawyers and is asked to attend more meetings about the road. A diabetic, her sugar level and blood pressure rise under the stress.

Kinship and Community-Level Dispute Resolution

One evening Lorna Gray Wolf's older sister unexpectedly visited Mrs. Runs Fast for no declared reason. They visited for several hours about "old times" until it was too late for Pat Gray Wolf to make the long drive home. Before settling in for the night on Mrs. Runs Fast's sofa, Pat gently urged her to "go along" with the easement and sign it, thus revealing the true intent of her visit.

What is also revealed is the significance of women's kin networks to bridge community factions and heal interfamily fissions. Lorna "sent" her sister, who "went along with what I wanted" for the road, to reach an informal agreement with Mrs. Runs Fast, who was preventing the agreement. This method of dispute resolution proved equally effective in Buffalo Bird Woman's day and was in fact at the heart of resolving the "trouble" surrounding *Idikita'c*'s fence Gilbert Wilson described.

In the intervening century, traditional dispute-settling mechanisms have been disrupted by the upheaval of relocations, the imposition of private-land allotments and the adoption of elected constitutional governments that replaced consensus-oriented tribal councils. The result of these forms of political reorganization has been to create complex structures of identity, where tribal members vie among competing interests for tribal lands. American Indian women activate their kin networks in attempts to bridge these factions, and by so doing, assert culturally meaningful and appropriate means of dispute resolution. The power of kinship ties becomes tested by one's willingness to comply with the request of kin.

At a critical juncture in the negotiations between the Runs Fast women and the Thunder Bay Cabin Owners Association, Mrs. Runs Fast asked me to testify in a hearing in tribal council chambers on behalf of the contested area and its value as a cultural historic site. Through my reflexive positioning as "anthropologist as sister," I was charged with acting out a kinship obligation using the public face of my professional clout. Similar to Pat Gray Wolf's intervention on behalf of her sister, my testimony reinforced my social responsibility to help bridge the factional divide, separating the interests of the tribal council, BIA representatives, cabin owners, and Indian landowners on behalf of my adoptive kinswomen. Mrs. Runs Fast, whose testimony reinforced the plea for cultural historic preservation measures and illuminated the implicit, yet direct, link between mythohistorical events and land, claimed:

> *I'm just a woman. There are others like me. . . . I don't have no man to help me, I'm just by myself . . . since the Garrison Dam. . . . I live in that place in town . . . just myself, with no place to even plant a garden. I have to go to the store for everything. . . . I don't want the [BIA] money. I told him*

[the superintendent] to take it back. That place is my grandmother's. That's where I grew up in that house. I don't know how many of you know that story about the [Boy] who came down and had powers to kill the snakes. He sawed off their heads . . . over there by [Bluff]. You can still see it there [even with the dam]. That's a Mandan story. My grandmother . . . was a Mandan.

Claims to cultural knowledge, like claims to kinship, assert a symbolic identity as a means to negotiate the law, yet remain outside the law. In this way, cultural identity is used to support claims to political and legal conflict. Kinship relations, which are themselves embedded in cultural knowledge, become activated as a means through which identity is acted out on a daily and continuing basis. In this context, Lorna Gray Wolf's trench along the road and Mrs. Runs Fast's testimony serve as acts of resistance to non-Indian strong-arm tactics and bureaucratic contracts (cf. Scott 1990). Moreover, although the two families arrive at different decisions about the easement, they both employ the same strategies of enlisting kin to bridge factions in their shared goal to retain cultural identity and control over tribal lands.

Informal mechanisms of dispute resolution mirror other forms of women's activities, such as exchange systems and leadership qualities. Whether conceptualized as "informal" and "formal," "ceremonial" and "political," "processual" and "categorical," the reasons for these co-occurring processes are embedded in the structural forces of historical change. Through time cultural codes of behavior have re-formed within the structural overlays of a cash economy, the effects of the IRA, and the Euro-American legal system. By crosscutting dichotomous spheres, women activate their defensive networks as a mediating buffer between dominant systems of economy, politics, and law on the one hand, and cultural sanctions on the other. In this way, the two systems become interdependent in that the one necessitates the other. Hence, "informal" economic strategies (described in chapters 2 and 3) become interpreted in the context of "formal" economies and lose their salience and meaning when attempts are made to formalize them. Likewise, extralegal forms of dispute resolution, specifically in the Thunder Bay case, arise in the context of legal disputes brought on by development strategies that undermine kinship imperatives. Tribal members get caught in the web of systemic change. On the one hand, the cultural system remains open to structural forces of change, which at the same time pull at the thread of the social fabric. This "pull" tightens social relations and frequently results in exacerbating intratribal tensions. In Buffalo Bird Woman's day, fission served as an extreme form of dispute resolution.[7] In the contemporary reservation context, appeasement through the sale of fee-simple allotments intensifies intratribal stratification while rendering a class of reservation residents landless on their own land.

When I interviewed an elder Hidatsa woman about her family history, I told her I would like to learn more about her family genealogy. She suggested I talk to other tribal members with whom she knew I had already developed associations. She then launched a diatribe against people who were adopted or married into the tribe as a way to get their names on land deeds. She also cited examples from when she worked at a nursing home on the reservation of elders who thanked their caretakers by naming them in land heirships. I took this message as twofold: First, as a way to ward off any future questioning on my part, and second, as a disclosure about the suspicions such inquiries about kinship and land rights raise. Disputes at the level of kinship and community have been commonplace since before Buffalo Bird Woman's day. In the larger political arena of national tribal politics and economic development, family-based concerns and disputes hinder economic development plans. The BIA upholds the legal trust relationship of tribal lands while it serves national political interests—even if those interests are represented by a few businessmen with ties to Congress. Government agencies, viewed by many residents as arms of colonial control, work with tribal governmental representatives to expedite economic development projects, especially those that are natural resource based, such as those that extract water, oil, gas, and land itself.

In the context of Thunder Bay, cultural identity is enacted as a defiant force that challenges the superstructural authority of the law without breaking it. Women-centered kin networks, such as those that connect the Runs Fast and Gray Wolf families, give shape to demands for self-determination. By comparison, in her work with Australian Aboriginal women's land claims, Diane Bell (1993) found that "aboriginal [*sic*] men of authority . . . spoke to white men of authority (lawyers, anthropologists, bureaucrats and clergy)" (p. 38). The decision-making bodies in Australia that establish the procedures and precedents for political and legal transactions bear striking resemblance to the overseeing bodies of American Indian affairs, where women's voices are trivialized or muted in the halls of mainstream institutions (MacKinnon 1987; Yellowbird 1994). To recoup their losses and retain control over their land and livelihood, Fort Berthold women walk in balance between kinship and community in their informal dealings, which in turn structure their national and cultural agenda.

Chapter 5

"All we needed was our gardens . . . "
Implications of State Welfare Reform on the Reservation Economy

Difference as uniqueness or special identity is both limiting and deceiving. If identity refers to the whole pattern of sameness within a human life, the style of a continuing me that permeates all the changes undergone, then difference remains within the boundary of that which distinguishes one identity from another. This means that *at heart* X must be X, Y must be Y, and X *cannot* be Y. Those who run around yelling that X is not X and X *can* be Y usually land in a hospital, a "rehabilitation" center, a concentration camp or a res-er-va-tion.

Minh-ha T. Trinh
Woman, Native, Other

(Re)Situated Lives

In resituating American Indian women's lives in the context of welfare reform and the reservation economy, several points converge to bring economic understandings in line with a politics of identity. First, the reservation as a "location of resistance" emerges as a site for class analysis. Conceptualizing the *community as worksite* (chap. 3) is one way to link community identity to this purpose. Patricia Albers (1996), in her analysis of wage work in Native North America, cautions that studies of American Indians and wage work should not replace representations of American Indians as "basket makers" with those of

105

"ironworkers." In the case of Mandan, Hidatsa and Arikara women, this reifi-
cation of the working-class slot ignores interlocking variables of race, class, and
gender, and the cultural aspects of class that point to tribal histories, specifici-
ties of place, and the interwoven relationships of kin that defy base levels of exploitation if only through the symbolic relations of production required for
maintaining "Indianness." Fort Berthold, despite the reconfiguration of communities in the face of the social upheavals of disease, reservationization, and
relocations, remains distinctly "Mandan," "Hidatsa," and "Arikara" (where
these three tribes come together in a shared national political identity as the
Three Affiliated Tribes). These multiple identities enforce, rather than frag-
ment, a sense of shared location in the wake of multiple oppressions.

Despite systematic extirpations of cultural life and the creation of racial
stereotypes, such as "lazy Indians," that anchor American Indians to the interests of capital (Moore 1996), they have not been excluded from the labor
process. In other words, exclusion from wage labor does not mean that people
do not work, as forays into the informal economy show, including most significantly the unremunerated work of women in the reservation economy.
From rations to welfare, these constructed dependencies have created more
complex survival strategies, such as the intersection of cash economies with
ceremonial work that inhere in *ceremonial relations of production.* Even during
historical intervals when American Indians have been excluded from formal
wage work, they nonetheless retain a class position. As a marker of identity,
class then becomes "unfixed." Just as identity itself can be permeated by shifting political and community boundaries, class mapping in any fixed way is in-
sufficient for locating the relationship of reservation Indians to shifting
capital. Class here is not an outcome of cultural life, delimiting a "no exit" option for members of poor communities or reinforcing a cycle of poverty
(Lewis 1961; cf. Aronowitz and DiFazio 1994). Rather, the cultural construction of class is informed by multiple dimensions of kinship, gender, and tribal
identity. Identity in relation to work is less about the nature of the work
women do (from craft work to factory work) than the social relations that govern it and the cultural matrices through which women view it. For instance,
Carol, a Mandan woman, spoke about her work in a microelectronics factory
in California:

> *[that work] . . . with all those copper wires and tiny things . . . was just
> like beadwork, and [so] it had something to do with me.*

Since the beginning of the twentieth century, American Indians have been conscripted to build railroads (Peters 1995; 2001), mine coal (Weiss 1984), clean houses, and assemble the machinery of war by exporting both labor power and capital away from the reservation economy. As illustrated in the previous chapters, Fort Berthold women combine a variety of paid jobs (working for tribal government, BIA, IHS, or the occasional start-up enterprises) with unpaid household labor, such as artistic production and preparations for the unending cycle of ceremonial activities. Despite the constant demand on women's productive labor, most of the work that women do remains unremunerated. Lack of jobs in the formal sector for both men and women hover at an average of 75 percent (BIA Aberdeen Area Office, 1991), with some improvement since the 1993 opening of the Four Bears Casino, which employs several hundred tribal members. Since the 1970s, reservation residents have also secured wage labor through the Northrop assembly plant situated on the edge of the reservation hub of New Town. Some tribal members have found wage work in distant cities, whereas others exercise their "exit" option by joining professional classes of artists, lawyers, educators, and medical doctors. Similar to other ethnic class communities, once individuals leave their class positioning, they rarely return home to live and work (Rodriguez 1990; cf. Wellman 1996).

Fort Berthold women participate in diversified ventures, often working for a wage, while actively participating in the daily rounds of social and ceremonial life. Many elders lament the loss of "traditional ways," yet sewing, beading, cooking, and preparing for ceremonies and feasts remain integral to sustaining cultural life. Although the specific forms may vary from former times (e.g., synthetic fabrics for ceremonial outfits, ceremonies conducted in a living room instead of an earthlodge), the *intent* and transformative nature of ritual presents a view of a culture still very much *practiced*, as Carol's transposition from beadwork to electronic assembly work demonstrates. Women's formal constructs of work in their response to work histories tend to reflect structural definitions that relate "work" to a wage. Yet the combined aspects of ceremonial labor, wage work, and other informal ventures amount to what one Hidatsa woman summarized: "It's hard work!"

In evaluating the work histories told here by Fort Berthold women, the "face value" of women's words, once inscribed, informs more than just a telling of tales about work, but produces a discursive text that must be read in relation to the structures outside the text itself. On the one hand, welfare policy is in itself a constructed narrative about the poor as marginalized and essentially Othered (Edelman 2002; Trinh 1989). However, the dialectic posed by the words of welfare recipients goes just part way in linking themselves to state structures by emphasizing only local practices. The critical aim to a testimonial approach such as the one taken here is to narrate the political economy in a way that accounts for the voices and "consequences of those on the bottom [to] help produce situated knowledges resistant to the homogenizing and marginalizing practices of top-down discourses" (Shram 1995, 75; cf. Moroney and Krysik 1998).

Working[2]

What I can remember of the old Indians in my time was that they were industrious people. They tilled their own gardens and always had a good supply of winter food. Cattle were given to them from the government in the beginning when reservation boundaries were settled. We all had a few head of cattle and it seemed to me that cattle survived fairly well on timberlands. With the exception of a few hard weeks in the winter months they probably were fed but otherwise they always survived, therefore, they had their meat, garden and produce and community activities. . . . At the time before the dam backed up the inundation of the Garrison reservoir just about everyone had a few head of cattle. . . . The potential good living is something I would like to elaborate on now. In these days our older people provided . . . they did not know what welfare was, what relief was at that time. John Stone (Mandan)[3]

Martha

Today Martha expects me and appears less harried by the community collections of shawls and goods than when she was last preparing for an event at the Catholic church. She was sent to Catholic mission school as a child and graduated when she was sixteen. Much of her informal life's work has been in relation to, if not in service of, the local parish. She speaks proudly of how the priest accepted a beaded vestment, thus signaling his acceptance of "Indian ways" by wearing an "Indian" garment. In the summer months between school terms, Martha held her first jobs in off-reservation towns that followed the work of her father.

I worked in a laundry in Bismarck because then my father was in Bismarck. He left and was working outside the reservation. [Then] I worked at the sanatorium. I don't know what they did with it now. It closed. [I had] just graduated and I worked in surgery. That doctor . . . really wanted me to go into medicine. I went to Haskell and they really trained you. It was a two-year business school. So as soon as I came from there I got a job. That's how I worked my way through college because I had Haskell behind me.

At that time, when I was young, they never referred to anybody by their name. It was always your brother, or here comes your child, or here comes your grandfather. So we knew who it was. But now for about two generations, that hasn't happened. That's why young kids don't know. They don't know their own relatives because of that. People have to work this eight-hour day thing. They don't have the time to be visiting like we used to. They are broken up.

As part of her community work efforts, Martha volunteers with an elder wellness project, a program partly devoted to teaching Native languages to children in the communities. Her community involvement is not "activist" in the political sense, yet her involvement with the National Congress of American Indians, the formation of an urban Indian center, and recent efforts to start a local NAIWA chapter indicates a community status that incorporates both informal and formal organizing skills (cf. Sacks 1988b). Interwoven with tales of the city where she held a steady job with the U.S. Department of Defense for more than twenty years, Martha's seasonal forays home continued to involve her in community rites—both at the Catholic church and within the kin community of her Mandan and Hidatsa relations. At various nodes along these webworks, she stepped in to parent several children, "nephews," who came to the east to go to school and live with her.

Narratives of child rearing embody the implicit forms of women's labor: they give voice to an ideology that is reflected by the gendered division of labor. For instance, in the inseparable spheres between family and work life, women assume child-rearing duties as their assigned roles as "carriers of culture"[4] and as transmitters of cultural values, including language (Medicine 1986). Generational positioning has much to do with women's perceptions of work, and consequently, the kind of work that they value.

Maude

The first job I ever had was back in 1937. When I first graduated the eighth grade, I thought I was really somebody. Right after I graduated the eighth grade I started working for a schoolteacher, housekeeping. It was just a country school, a grade school in the Shell Creek district there. I worked there in the summer and fall and then I went to Montana [and] worked in a motel. [After that] we went out to Fort Totten. I met him [my husband] over there and he followed me back [to North Dakota] and I came back to the reservation and he stayed over there at work. And while I was working, he went down to my uncle's house. That's where I got trapped! Anyway, I went to visit my daughter in Washington and I went to work over there too for two weeks. That was in '69. I just went over there to visit and, crazy me, I told my daughter, "Let's go look for a job." Different places, you know, we gave that motel number [where they were staying] and when we got back they said, "There's a phone message for you." I went and answered it and I got the job. So then the next day I went to work—at a cleaner's. So I worked there for two weeks. I did fast work, and I was way ahead. And she liked my work. One day I went in and she said, "Come on in. We asked you to be here early, I'm going to show you how we get things going." So she showed me the back room, where to get the steams and everything set up already. But I called home one night and here my girl said, "They're having a big flood over there [in North Dakota]." I told her [Maude's boss], "I want to go home. They're having a big flood over there." I don't know why but that evening I came home [to Fort Berthold]. I never got my check [from work]. I just came home, and then I went to work for different employers there. Actually I had to go out and work because I didn't have [any money]. Well, I did get a little lease money but it wasn't much to make a living on. So I just worked here and there.

Eventually, Maude left Fort Berthold again and moved to another state with her daughter:

I said, "I'll go with you and I'll look for a job down there." We were down there two weeks and here in about a couple of days I got a job in a bowling alley washing dishes. I took [the kids] down there with me. It was okay, but see my sister and I were staying together. She didn't work but her husband worked and I worked. So we were paying the rent. She was paying half and I was paying half and I had my kids there. And one day we were going to eat and here we only had two chairs. No, one chair. There was only one chair in the house and her boy. Well I bought the groceries. I was the one that was working so I went out and bought the groceries. Lunch meat and stuff. And here I had it ready on the table. "Okay, you kids come and eat," I

*said. He [the boy] ran for that chair . . . [a fight ensued over the chair], so
the next day I went to work. I got my check that time. I called him [a friend]
and told him that these kids wanted to come back [home]." "Oh, okay, I'll
be over there tomorrow he said." . . . I came back and I moved in with him,
and it didn't work out so I rented the house and I moved out.*

Back on the reservation again, Maude got involved with an economic
development effort to teach pottery making to local women. A man who was
the friend of a local white businessman led the workshops. The workshops
were aimed at engendering self-sufficiency through small-scale crafts production, similar to the EARN project described in chapter 3, and reminiscent of
New Deal policies. This time, however, private funds backed the project, and
in this way, the pottery workshops closely resemble the welfare-to-work models that attempt to assign "culturally appropriate" work to poor women, much
like the early reservation era efforts of the Indian Arts and Crafts Board to
reteach beadwork and other sewing skills to American Indian women. Essentialist notions of American Indian women as nimble-fingered craftspeople
translate from crafts to factory work, even as women internalize these images
of themselves, as Carol demonstrated in her description of the California microelectronics plant, and as women's labor around the world has been simi-
larly targeted (Bulakishnan 2002; Enloe 1990; Nash and Fernandez-Kelly
1983; Ong 1987). In contrast to Helen's testimony of finding work satisfaction
at the Northrop assembly plant, Maude experienced it as the most stressful
work she had ever done.

*I walked into something that I didn't even know a thing about. . . . I
asked [what they manufactured there] but they never told me. . . . There's
different things, like I make, but there was one thing that looks like a toilet
seat. They call it a heat exchanger. That goes in an airplane. That tip is kind
of a round thing. "It fits in there," they said. And the heat could make it either warmer or cooler. That's why they call it a heat exchanger. . . . They
make all kinds of things. Most of the PC boards and stuff. I don't know what
they do with that. Really if it comes down to right where it goes, I don't
know. I was just there to put them together. . . . And there's another one too.
It's called a guidance system. It's kind of a harness like. When they're out at
sea, it tells you how far up or down you go or something like that. That's
what made me really worried. [The trainer from California] was telling
me, it's a guidance system that you'll know how far below the sea. She was
only there one week! There was two of us . . . she was showing how to do it.*

I was just sitting by looking. And this [other] girl was working at it. And the second week she [the trainer] didn't come back, and this [other] girl said: "well Maude, I think it's up to you." The girl didn't come back either. She didn't even show up!

  She never did come. So I was stuck with it. The first time when she did it, I didn't pay much attention to it. . . . And then I thought about it, "Gee, if they were out in the sea and they got lost, it would be my fault." And you know what, that really made me scared. . . . I was so worried, I would go into the bathroom about fifteen, twenty minutes apart. And I would pray. And I would be in there and think how "my head feels hot." That's how worried I was. I've never been so worried in all my life.

The kind of work Maude described in the Northrop assembly plant in the 1970s presaged the boom in microelectronic assembly work that would later employ a new generation of migrants in urban areas. The effects of the postindustrial shift on women and their families only recently came under academic scrutiny in the 1990s (Kaplan, Alarcón, and Moallem 1999; Stacey 1990). For many American Indian women who trained for work through the American Indian Relocation and Vocational Assistance Act, changes to a postindustrial era of high-tech computer-based skills left them largely unprepared to meet the demands of new job requirements.

Judy

Judy went on relocation with the first wave of urban migrants in the 1950s. Her husband got work in Chicago, and the lure of life away from the reservation drew her like a wide-eyed girl to big city life. In many respects, Judy adjusted well to urban life, and through a series of midlevel jobs she worked her way into her first sales job at a major department store. Like other women who left home for wage work in distant cities, her story is rife with the isolation of being an American Indian in a foreign place, a stranger in her own land. Displaced from their networks of kin, many women endured their loneliness in silence, especially when marriages failed or became abusive. Despair was sometimes the driving force in returning home—to which testimonies of return migration attest (Berman n.d.; Kemnitzer, Willard, et al. 1971; cf. Lobo and Peters 2001). Similar to Chicana work-based friendship networks (viz. Zavella 1987), Judy developed relationships with white women at work, relationships that she claims helped her to dispel negative stereotypes about whites.

*When we first married, we had our oldest one [child] here . . . and he
[her husband] looked for a job. He couldn't find no job. He was working on
the farm, and that was what he made. He made $30 a week and that was
what went for milk because I had no breast milk for my oldest one. So I had
to be on canned milk. So most of the money he made went to the milk. We
had it hard here. . . . We did get those [commodities], but it wasn't much.
Just the two of us, and then we stayed at his mother's place and all her children lived with her. So it was like, you were lucky to get a serving.*

*He had a brother that came back on relocation. . . . My folks didn't want
me to go [on relocation] because it was so far away. But I went. I didn't get
lonesome because I was quite young. But I got used to it. I was afraid of the
city. . . . After the divorce . . . I went back to Chicago. I thought if I worked
here I might not get them [kids]. So I got a baby-sitter and I found a job at
the department store. This is where I learned all of what I know now. It's helping me now. It's kind of something. That's where I worked. That was my first
job. I had to learn how to run a cash register and sell merchandise.*

Judy worked her way up the managerial chain of command to become
an assistant buyer in a major department store. She now runs a small craft outlet, housed in the tribal museum, where she has assumed, by virtue of her job
training, the taking of inventories, producing condition reports, and the la-
beling tasks of collections management. In a community with little infrastruc-
ture to support the requirements of museum development, Judy carved a
niche for herself by combining her formal training with the informal business
of handicraft production, sale, and exchange.

Anna

Anna breaks from her secretarial job at the tribal administration building as
we follow the noon rush to the bowling alley cafeteria where we look for a
table as far away as possible from the watchful community gaze. When I last
interviewed Anna she was an unemployed mother, working part-time as a
baby-sitter. Now with another child on the way, she's looking at her job with
measured glances to the clock. She is one of the youngest women I interviewed; she was only nineteen when we met. That was more than a few years
ago, and we've since become good friends and family. Accustomed in the
early days to her wilder friends' invitations to joyride across the Four Bears
Bridge, I now take comfort in relaxing in her homey trailer, helping myself

to soda, and now refilling my glass as our interview from earlier in the day continued:

>   *I went to business administration [at college], but I wasn't serious enough about it. At that time, all I did was party. And then when you do that, everything else just doesn't fall into place. So I just came back. My first job was in the male [dominated industry of] construction. Flagging up north here. It was only, I think, for maybe a month. I didn't mind the work at that time. No kids, you go to work. You make a lot of good money. You put in lots of hours. . . . I had my aunt out there. She's my dad's sister. She's the one that I'm closest to of all his sisters.*

>   *I was twenty when I had my first kid. That's when I was working for that job training partnership, that JTPA [Job Training Program Administration]. The JTPA program paid the wage of $3.25 per hour and usually they were under a work experience program, but there were other [programs] too, on-the-job training. . . . [Then] we got our per cap[ita payment]. Mine was 10,000 [dollars]. You just get a check in the mail on your twenty-first birthday. One lump sum to do with whatever you want to do. In some ways it's bad. You don't know anything. You're very immature. Really, what did I know? I bought myself a car first. I was just getting started. I got myself a car for 6 or 8,000 [dollars]. I bought my dad a horse trailer, something he's always wanted. Then I put some in the bank for school. Then I went on a trip to Yellowstone. It was fun. Why not? I don't ever regret it either. It's something that a lot of people don't get the chance to do. Just to pick up and say, "I think I'll go to Yellowstone!" and just go.*

>   *When one of us [she and her husband] wasn't working, we'd get unemployment. We've been blessed somehow, because one of us had always been working. And I thank God and I knock on wood that we've both been working. It hasn't been without, boom, sudden cash-flow stopped. [We used to] get WIC. Women, Infant[s] and Children Program. Where you get your child's immunization. That's free. They supply you with nutritional food. The basics like milk, juice, peanut butter, eggs, beans. You get checks . . . for the store that you shop at. And you go in and you just get those supplies and that's it. . . . A case of formula almost costs $70. We haven't really needed commodities, I guess.*

In the process of interviewing Anna, she reflected on how the interview experience made her think about things that she never thought of before. For instance, when I posed my inflated community development question: "If you had $1 billion to spend on community development, how would you spend it?" she answered simply, "On kids." Her idea—to start a reservation-based foster-care program—actually came to pass during the course of my fieldwork when the Tribal Administration built and housed the Casey Foundation foster-care agency that worked with reservation families to keep American Indian children within the community. Josie Chase, a tribally enrolled member of Fort Berthold, directed the program, and later went on to Washington D.C., to serve on the National Congress of American Indians. By Anna's wishes and Josie's accomplishments, we see how the grassroots concerns of individual women rooted in the familistic values of kinship hold the potential to link community issues to national politics.

Linda

Linda stretches her legs out across the bed that we share as a couch for interview purposes and for "just kicking back" on a cloudy July day. Having lived off the reservation with a military husband, she's seen a fair amount of the world abroad, and an even greater amount up close at home, where she shares a house with her mother, husband, daughter, and several grandchildren, all "brothers" and "sisters"—classificatory kin, "Indian way." A college graduate, she encourages my chronicle of daily life on the reservation. Through the combination of GI money, unemployment, and a teacher's income, her household members pool funds and shuffle the balance of cash and goods for daily subsistence and ceremonial occasions.

> We don't qualify [for commodities]. My mom works as a teacher. I never lived on the reservation long enough to have a job here. My first real job would have been in South Dakota. I started out as an assembly worker for Control Data. A hardware for military aircraft. They had a training program where I went to school. Employees went to school at their own expense. . . . I worked my way up to the assistant shift supervisor before leaving. I did a lot with my husband being in the military. I did a lot of volunteer work. Family services, Red Cross, and NCO [non-commissioned officers] wives . . . a lot of community service type work.

The only time I ever really ran into culture shock [was coming back to the reservation]. Instead of walking around the block to buy something that I forgot, you had to go thirty-seven miles. Trying to get a phone connected. If you could produce an ID card, Indian ID card, you weren't charged tax. But yet your deposit was higher. When [her non-Indian husband] went in and was going to get the phone, there was no security deposit, and then he told them that he had an Indian wife. They said bring in her ID card and they'll be tax exempt. So he brought in my ID card and we had to put down [a] $250 deposit for the phone!

[As for the most satisfying work,] I would have to bring it home, domestic. That's watching my daughter grow. That and I guess how you go into a job. If you're going to go in with a miserable attitude, then it's going to be a miserable job. If you go in as an adventure and try to build it from the bottom up, then it makes it. As for jobs, I've never had one that was miserable. And I've always liked all of them because I made them into something that was mine.

In addition to her range of volunteer work and parenting, Linda also holds certifications in cosmetology and auto mechanics, and she once worked as a truck driver for the American Red Cross. She is unabashed about her admiration for men's work, which she proudly accomplishes with great skill. In fact, we joked about how between the two of us, we could fashion a traditional gendered division of labor. Linda's work experiences, combining sewing and beading her daughter's dance outfits, helping a brother prepare for the Sun Dance ceremony, working on cars, and general handiwork around the house, defy gender stereotypes about what gets to count as women's work. Industries that target women's work as an extension of craft production will miss these diverse talents that many women have, as well as the academic knowledge that women with college degrees hold with no local "market" outside of the tribal college and a very few specialized positions reservationwide.

As Linda's testimony and work experiences point out, the distinction between the state and the market is one that is not readily made by policy reformers. Furthermore, the welfare state has succumbed to the market in such large measure that it is equally critical to distinguish the welfare state from the welfare *system*, especially because it is the latter that government policy makers critique without taking into account the failure of the state to provide for its citizenry (Piven in Schram 1995). Other distinctions in policy efforts that frequently go unaccounted for include relationships of "rights" to "justice" (Barry 1990), especially for American Indians, where government provisioning remains a negotiated treaty right. Furthermore, and most relevant to the exposition of American Indian women's economic interests, even in the renarrating of welfare policy, the gender neutrality of both liberal and Marxist political theory ignores the fact that most public debates about welfare center on women and children.

Feminist scholars who apply a "gender lens" to work and welfare research move theory forward by breaking down false dichotomies and help to reverse the gaze of the state on its subjects (Abromowitz 1988; Scott 1998). The work American Indians perform is similar to that performed by other women of color, in that the intersection of race and gender becomes masked by the ways in which women are drawn into particular forms of wage labor by necessity. Although the kind of work American Indian women do—from domestic labor to service work—may share similar features of other working-class women, the cautionary note offered earlier by Albers (1983) is mitigated by culture-based expressions of work and family life. Exactly how these differ from other women's work experiences would be a test of the ways that ceremonial relations of production have parallel constructions in other communities.

Policy Revisited

When analyzed over time, economic development policies are the flip side of welfare reform. Where local economies intersect with state-level prerogatives, women most often negotiate between family ideologies and development imperatives. For American Indian communities, these policies run a parallel track to larger federal reform movements—from the Jacksonian era of forced relocation and dispensation of rations, to the War on Poverty campaigns of the Johnson administration, which ushered in the era of self-determination. Since the nineteenth century allotment of Native lands, the ideological problem with federal interventions in the reservation economy rests with an economic value of privatization that runs counter to tribal values of land use and kinship (Cornell 2000; Cornell and Kalt 1992; Ward and Snipp 1996).

The discourse of self-determination politics relied on treaties as the precedent and foundation on which legislative ground was won in the earlier days of Indian activism, especially in land rights and religious freedom. The inaugural days of the self-determination movements drew increasing attention to women's claims, which in turn grew out of land rights and resource litigation in Indian Country nationwide. At the same time, treaties have proven to be the critical endpoint for staking legal claims to sovereignty by situating American Indians within a wider body of international law (Strickland 1998).

Through a series of U.S. Supreme Court decisions, treaties established Tribes as simultaneously "domestic" and "dependent" *nations*[5]—a contradiction with which Tribes and legal scholars continue to grapple. The result has been a type of "quasi-sovereignty," which until recently offset state jurisdiction over federally recognized Tribes (Goldberg-Ambrose 1997; Wunder 1999). The relationship between American Indian Tribes and the U.S. government continues to be outlined by the terms defined within this federal-trust relationship (Biolsi 1995; Wilkins 1997).

The federal-trust relationship is a contradictory one, marked by vacillations in federal Indian policy between isolation on the one hand and assimilation on the other, and shaped by a unique body of federal Indian law that recognizes the inherent decision-making rights of Tribes over their own internal affairs (Clark 1994; Deloria and Wilkins 1999) while subjecting them to federal oversight in matters of land, natural resources, housing, health care, and economic development. In these ways, the federal-trust relationship sets American Indians apart from other U.S. ethnic minorities by holding fiduciary and fiscal responsibilities administered by federal agencies to federally recognized Tribes. Until the passage of the Personal Responsibility and Work Opportunity Reconciliation Act of 1996 (P.L. 104–193) or Welfare Reform Act, responsible agencies included the BIA, as the federal arbitrator between the U.S. government and American Indian Tribes; HUD, which administers block grants to Tribes for reservation housing; the IHS; and a host of federal welfare programs not unique to American Indians, such as GA, replaced by TANF, SSI, food stamps, and commodity food programs. In addition, the Indian Employment, Training and Related Services Demonstration Act of 1992 (PL 102–477) allows Tribes to combine federal programs into a comprehensive formula for implementation and program distribution.[6] These programs help to define aspects of the welfare system, which, as discussed earlier, functions apart from the welfare state.

According to the terms of the Welfare Reform Act, local states (as opposed to the federal government) have new authority to request and administer funds, and "at their option" may include tribal family assistance programs in their numbers for requesting block grants. Tribes may therefore opt to administer their own service delivery programs—one of the key premises of devolution that seems to hold promise for tribal sovereignty (Pandy et. al. 1999, 2000). However, irrespective of disbursement procedures, the most direct effect on American Indian communities, both on and off the reservation, will continue to be felt as a result of new caps on spending and time limits for TANF recipients, and the consolidation of nutrition programs, such as food stamps, WIC programs, and school lunch programs. These new cuts slice into the reservation economy, where contradictory policies have forced a delicate balance between formal and informal economies (Pickering 2000). New program caps and time limits that reduce welfare rolls without eliminating conditions of poverty threaten to undercut the ways that American Indians have come to combine household resource strategies with various forays into wage work. In these ways, welfare reform is an extension of contradictory federal policies that have served to uphold or dismantle federal-trust responsibilities through time.

Since the advent of treaties, federal Indian policy has guided social rearrangements of Native communities—from reservations to relocation and urbanization programs. By limiting or eliminating federal oversight, welfare reform goes to the heart of legal doctrine that gives Tribes their unique status vis-à-vis federal programs: the federal-trust relationship.

Subsequent policies of social welfare reform tactics followed federal Indian policy through its vacillations between isolation and assimilation. In either case, the alienation of Native lands has always been the cornerstone of federal interventions. As noted in chapter 1, the first legislative attempt at privatization of tribal holdings came about through the implementation of the Dawes Allotment Act of 1887, which ceded fee-simple property rights to individual Indians deemed "competent" by a U.S. court of law. The competency clause raises itself as an interesting specter in the light of 1990s welfare reform policy, which allows some Tribes to manage their own welfare rolls providing they are "qualified" to do so (as stipulated by the Balanced Budget Act of 1997). The ideology of "competency" embedded in paternalistic policies that grant "sovereignty" with federal aplomb and take it away with state sanction, mirror the requirements laid out by termination policies of the 1950s, which ended federal-trust responsibility to Tribes deemed "qualified" to manage their own affairs.

For American Indians, the swiftness of federal reform by the stroke of a pen is not new. Although some social welfare researchers suggest that the new options give some Tribes more control over distribution of welfare benefits, what the changes echo, according to women I asked, is "Termination all over again." In part, this sentiment suggests that welfare reform, constructed in a political mood of ruthless cuts to subsistence benefits, delivers a direct blow to American Indian women, who have chiseled a fine line of survival through a package of benefits outlined by treaties and legally protected by the federal-trust relationship.

In the context of welfare reform, termination, as an underlying policy, continues to point like a double-edged sword: on the one hand, it translates to swift cuts from the welfare rolls through TANF rules and shortened time limits, and on the other hand, by devolving welfare block grants to Tribes through states, it extinguishes federal-trust responsibilities once guaranteed by treaty in exchange for the taking of Native lands. Precisely how reservation communities intend to cope with deep cuts to their economies forces a critical examination into the ways in which community members—especially women who receive the bulk of welfare payments for dependent children—strategize to make ends meet. In particular, American Indian women continue to shoulder the responsibilities of balancing work and family life due to the structural effects of increases in female-headed households and the interhousehold exchange cycles that radiate out from women-centered kin networks.

A main manifestation of cultural practices is the ongoing regulation of kinship solidarity as a central component to both "subsistence" and "sovereignty." In this light, I have discussed the importance of differentiating between matrifocal households founded on matrilineal kinship principles and "female-headed households," which signal poverty to social welfare observers (Jordan 1992; Mink 1999). From an anthropological perspective, these two faces of matrifocality are not always easily distinguishable. Therefore, a careful assessment of both cultural factors and social constraints needs to be a part of sound implementation of policies. Again, a historical understanding of key policy turns enables a consideration of the possible pitfalls and strengths of current and future legislation.

By focusing on American Indian women's work, the question, "What counts as work?" is raised as a new vantage point for considering (and contesting) what welfare-to-work really means for communities—especially if policy implementations were to allow for the various kinds of work that people do. For instance, if devolution of funds to Tribes included tribal interpretations of welfare-to-work programs (whereby tribal members define their own work activities), then a new form of tribal *control* over tribal resources (i.e., labor power) might indeed lend itself to enhancing tribal sovereignty.

Welfare-Based Economies Prior to 1996 Welfare Reform

The Personal Responsibility and Work Opportunity Reconciliation Act of 1996 effectively replaced Aid to Families With Dependent Children (AFDC) and formally ended the principal federal welfare law that operated as an open-ended entitlement from the federal government to qualifying families, especially families defined as mothers and children. In chapter 3 I outlined what some of the general aid programs consisted of prior to welfare reform, and how subsequent to the legislation, many programs continue to be cut in compliance with overall federal budget cuts to welfare recipients. Since the early reservation period when commodities were first introduced to Native communities, bureaucratic welfare programs became income options that Fort Berthold women managed and integrated into their household and community activities.

The figures outlined in this book show only ten years of data, representing the impossibility of making ends meet on government assistance alone. Yet without this assistance, many reservation households would be unable to support themselves at all. Failed job training programs and out-migration flows prior to welfare reform offer no substantive options for generating long-term economic stability for reservation economies. Shuffling income options and pooling kinship resources remain tested strategies that hold together the various strands of social life and livelihood. These include forays into wage work, when it exists, and the ingenuity of informal economic tactics. The long-term effects of welfare reform threaten to disrupt formal and informal economies where they intersect, and undercut the delicate balance struck by reservation women.

With every new policy era, American Indians adjust to structural constraints, but not without cost. While American Indians have always been asked to pay the price for shifts in national policies, at the same time they manage to imbue new ways of making a living with cultural meanings that reconceptualize ideologies of "work" away from its association to a wage in the formal sector. The informal economy has been understood to serve this purpose in other communities whose members subsist on the margins of the political economy (Nash 1993; Pickering 2000; Stoller 1996).

As outlined earlier through the overview of federal Indian policies, "welfare reform" reads as a policy of state contraction that is consistent with historical trends to isolate, assimilate, remove, and disband tribal control over tribal resources, including labor power. Whereas ceremonial relations of production mitigate against culture loss, the fragility of the reservation economy is not impervious to economic and cultural harm. Globalization of production—from Northrop's expansion at Fort Berthold to the international export trade in American Indian goods—conscripts Indian labor in new forms while cutting economic assistance programs in violation of the federal-trust relationship. The result is a renewed confusion with respect to the "sovereign dependency" of Tribes by allowing for neither (cf. P. Deloria 1998).

Implications for Welfare Reform on the Reservation Economy

By acknowledging American Indians' contributions to wage labor and stressing the importance of American Indian women's ceremonial work, the previous chapters show the ways that formal and informal economies have become enmeshed within both economic and cultural life in reservation communities. Ceremonial relations of production provide a mechanism for underscoring these interrelationships and reveal their central role in spreading the risks of survival across households and community factions.

Development enterprises that intervene in the reservation economy by attempting to formalize informal activities have had limited success, especially where cultural conceptions of work, both as a process and an objective, clash with profit incentives that target individuals without regard for the family economy. Welfare-to-work programs are therefore not new or unique in their approach to target individuals for meager economic incentives. Nor is the Welfare Reform Act without precedent in its inadequate measures to protect Indian child welfare. During a 1996 address to the national governors conference, President Clinton commented: "[I believe] the biggest shortcoming . . . of the bill I helped write, the Family Support Act of 1988 . . . was that we didn't do enough in the child welfare area." Despite this statement, and recent amendments to the American Indian Child Welfare Act of 1978, the Welfare Reform Act of 1996 does not once mention this important piece of protective legislation. Target legislation, such as the American Indian Women and Families Act of 1994, cannot begin to address with $2 million in appropriations the purported billions of dollars in net "savings" that the Welfare Reform Act gouged from its programs.

The rhetoric of welfare reform continues to reproduce an ideology of self-sufficiency while doing little to tackle the material conditions that rein-force economic and racial inequalities (Funiciello 1993; Hirshwann and Liebert 2000; Quadagno 1994). This rhetoric is familiar territory to the sur-vivors of Termination Era policies. For example, as a test case for termination, the Wisconsin Menominee Tribe broke up tribal holdings into corporate shares that left them little else in the way of housing and other subsistence needs. In this way, "self-sufficiency" stands in for "self-determination" in pol-icy terms, but only in the limited sense of compliance with federal guidelines. Furthermore, federal job training programs do not keep pace with industry demands, and where they do, it is only to offset the cost of labor production.

Ceremonial relations of production enables communities to come to terms with the interrelationships of the informal economies of both men's and women's work and the formal economies of wage and welfare systems. These interrelationships have proven to be intricately woven into the reser-vation economy as a whole. Moreover, some researchers predict that urban Indians subject to two-year time limits for TANF (unlike their reservation relatives) will find themselves relying increasingly on extended kin for assis-tance, thus straining already limited resources. At Fort Berthold, this caution was noted in an assessment of welfare-to-work programs, by which program evaluators stated that: "If large numbers of [tribal members] return to the reservation because their TANF 'time limit' is (or is about to be) exhausted, the already inadequate resources and associated services are likely to be over-whelmed" (TAT Site Visit Report, April 2000). By describing how kin net-works operate beyond the reservation boundaries (e.g., Laura's quilt for a bus ticket), I suggest that these structural interdependencies extend across cul-tural geographies—where urban and rural remittances flow between primary and subsidiary households.

Although these flows can be said to mirror the strategies of other mi-grant populations, the twist in Indian Country remains, as it always has, that cultural commitments to life-cycle events (from funerals to public honoring ceremonies) require the movement of cash and goods from cities to reserva-tions along the contours of women's kin networks. As shown in chapter 4, these defensive networks that protect communities from outside intervention (as in the Thunder Bay case) potentially can be activated to serve larger na-tional political agenda. National organizations, such as the National Council of American Indians (NCAI), and institutional associations, such as the American Indian Higher Education Consortium (AIHEC), help to redress community conditions by working on an agenda with common concerns, such as the impact welfare policies have on American Indian communities.

Following from Victor Turner (1982), it is in the liminal space that lies "betwixt and between" economic and ceremonial, public and private, formal and informal, reservation and city, that ceremonial relations of production allow simultaneously for economic adjustments to the macroeconomy while reinforcing kinship and social relations that remain at the heart of cultural membership and continuity. In effect, they provide a buffer to conditions of abject poverty, and in this way cast a defensive network across families and community members (March and Taqqu 1986; Stack 1997). These defensive networks can be "activated" in times of need, such as the proactive stance of the Runs Fast women to protect their land rights, to the mobilization efforts of activists and political figures in public leadership roles.

What welfare-to-work rhetoric demands is a critical examination of what counts as "work," and how race, class, and gender assumptions are built into welfare reform tactics and economic development schemes. Furthermore, privatization of social services, such as the transition to privatized food banks in the United States at the turn of this twenty-first century, will continue to see parallel effects in Indian Country, such as cuts in commodity distribution and community programs, including the Meals on Wheels subsidies that provide food to the elderly. Initial cuts to these programs have already created a crisis in social services administration in some reservation communities (p.c., Harvey). As former White Mountain Apache Tribal Chairman Ronnie Lupe stated in an editorial to the tribal newspaper *The Fort Apache Scout*:

> *The White Mountain Apache Tribe did not create welfare, the federal government did. So if it's the federal government's intent to dismantle welfare, then it should provide opportunities for welfare recipients rather than throwing them out on the street.* (cited in Stromwall et al. 1998, 7)

Some Fort Berthold women have described recent cutbacks to Indian programs as a backlash to sovereignty movements and punishment for the perceived success, however uneven, of Indian gaming as a component of economic self-sufficiency. In this spirit, the Personal Responsibility and Work Opportunity Reconciliation Act of 1996 reads as a new kind of "treaty"—a contract with (Native) America of sorts—that reaffirms power relations between policy makers and their constituents. What reformers of the welfare system do not concede is the failure of the welfare state to meet the needs of its citizenry. At the turn of a new century in U.S. policy, the failure of the state appears to be leashed on the market as individuals compete for increasingly privatized resources.

An understanding of how social spaces have become simultaneously privatized, enclosed, and subject to surveillance has long been critical to understanding how federal Indian policy shapes the reservation economy. The results of federal interventions stand as an artifact of these policies. In a similar vein, Benedict Anderson (1991) has argued for nationalism as a kind of "cultural artifact," and one that continues to transform as the cultural spaces themselves become more scattered (Grewal and Kaplan 1994). Although simultaneous practices of containment and dispersal appear as obvious contradictions, the contradictions are the logical outcomes of a vacillating, yet systematic, federal policy aimed at the consolidation of land and wealth ever since the 1880s Removal Era. This aim is nothing new to U.S. social history. However, the tactics employed in Indian Country result in new social formations created by women-centered kin networks and ceremonial relations of production. Together these social mechanisms reinforce a new kind of "nationality" (i.e., Tribes as Nations), especially with respect to cultural identity as an emblematic marker of tribal sovereignty.

Likewise, in social theory building, we must remain mindful of oscillating trends. Since the late 1950s through the 1960s, the "culture of poverty" thesis first put forth in the ethnographic work of anthropologist Oscar Lewis continues to assert itself as a "cycle of policy" that is best exemplified through the federal oversight that regulates various economic development and assistance programs in Indian Country. Elsewhere, following from Lewis's thesis that poverty is generationally transmitted and becomes culturally embedded, the 1965 Moynihan Report upheld the view that poverty was an unending "cycle," and that furthermore, the responsibility and blame lay with African American women, for and about whom the policy was drafted. Since the 1970s, anthropologists and social critics have systematically refuted this thesis (most notably, Stack 1975), yet so-called cultural causes persist as a way to explain poverty without a firm acknowledgment of the structural factors that impinge daily and historically on the economically marginalized—the poor, the Other.

By (re)situating a small community of American Indian women in the context of both their daily lives and the government policies that constrain and shape specific strategies, I hope this book will lend valuable understandings

Figure 5.1. Three Affiliated Tribes and the Community Celebrate Wellness.

about other communities where the interlocking dimensions between state sanctions and cultural practices inform the outcomes of policy.

Through a consideration of the impact of welfare reform on the reservation economy, the inextricable relationship between land, identity, and work becomes more clear. Examining past policies in conjunction with local realities helps to illuminate not only economic conditions, but also the social possibilities for change. Lydia, a Hidatsa elder who served as a national organizer for the NAIWA, commented on the importance of recollecting the past to build a strong foundation for the future:

> *I think on every reservation people have been looking back into their pasts, trying to integrate into their lives some of the more old customs and traditions people were forced to lay aside. I think here [at Fort Berthold], the greatest trauma was when people were forced to leave their bottomlands . . . when we lived down there, very little had to do with cash. [We] never had a problem with water . . . we had our own home and garden . . . hauling wood and coal . . . no one was lazy, we managed to survive. In the process [since then], there's been a lot of changes. Back then they didn't know what welfare was!*

In the old days—from the days of Buffalo Bird Woman to the childhood memories of women such as Andrea, Carol, Nancy, and Maude—gardens were the means to self-sufficiency. For Fort Berthold women born before the Garrison Dam, the Missouri River fed this possibility for decades of reservation life. When I asked Charlene, a Shell Creek elder, when they introduced the commodity programs, she answered, "Oh, just lately." This measure of time in decades compares to the way of life that preceded it for centuries. For a younger generation of women, the stories of their foremothers feed their hopes for the future, and their drive to revitalize their cultural way of life.

Women's informal and ceremonial activities meet the market at the borderzones of the reservation economy, a localized space of generational and tribal diversity. Within this newly created space, Mandan, Hidatsa, and Arikara women continue to thread their own designs across the social fabric—through their art, language, and shared responsibilities as keepers of land and kinship, and workers for social justice.

Afterword

From my first forays into Indian Country and in the years now since I have lived in the community of Fort Berthold, new developments in social welfare, cultural studies, and American Indian life have taken shape. At the same time, many of the fundamental themes raised by this book remain, not only for reservation communities, but as more general applications to understanding the processes of how power relations inform identity, and how the state exercises controls over everyday life. In the context of one reservation setting, I have attempted to show how forces of power relations are not structured *outside* of cultural practices, but permeate them in ways that lend new dimensions and meanings to people's lives. One way of tracing relations of power is through exchange, and this has been my focus. Marx (1867 [1978]) pointed out how power relations function through the arm of commodity exchange, and how the desire for objects (and how value is ascribed to them) becomes a form of commodity fetishism. Mauss (1923) elaborated on the various forms of exchange in his treatise, *The Gift*, and Annette Weiner (1992) shed feminist and anthropological light on the critical relationships that allow members of kin-based societies to "keep-while-giving." The points I draw together from these now classic texts include context-specific ideas of use value and aesthetics, and the generalizing principle that goods move not only through whole systems of circulation and exchange, but sometimes beyond them. Anthropologists have used these concepts of exchange as analytical fodder for decades, yet the *combination* of function and form with active and inventive resistance strategies gives rise to new ways of thinking about the flow of goods both within and outside of reciprocal cycles of exchange. Hence, I develop the idea of *ceremonial relations of production* as one way to think about how symbolic relations link up with economic relations in ways that are simultaneously situated and represented.

Social objects, like cultural identities, are "representative" because they are partial representations of whole systems of movements (of goods, money, and people) and forms of articulation (class, race/ethnicity, gender, age, culture). By extension, any presentation of social life is in its own right only a partial distillation of knowledges and social realities. I suggest this in the beginning of the book by admitting that even narrative testimonies are self-censored, edited and re-presented. In anthropology, ethnography as narrative form has shaped a large body of academic and popular impressions and discourses. It is one way of telling a story.

The story of colonial and postcolonial interventions is an old tale respun through the histories of produced subjects within world systems. As remarked on by a Native American participant at a 1999 welfare reform conference: "American Indians have been dealing with federal laws and policies for more than one hundred and fifty years, so welfare reform is nothing new." In short, this book underscores this point. The particular disruptions caused by changes to formal and informal economies lend themselves to new forms of participation, resistance, and identity formation (e.g., "welfare warriors"), which in turn rely on the steady pulse that flows through social relations. In these ways, the circle of goods—from cash to quilts to Pampers—shapes everyday life, even as it redefines it. At the heart of these dislocations (from social place and space), lies a conservative notion of collectivity.

I have shown how Fort Berthold women reconfigure community across complex arrays of social networks. However, I now caution that we not substitute an understanding about the effects of social fragmentation for a romanticized notion that overlooks the ways in which community members become complicit with capitalist interventions. Within this notion lies a temptation to essentialize kinship as the cornerstone for social cohesion, but this overstates the ways in which family members can drain, as well as sustain, family resources. What is required is a much more systematic interrogation into what we mean by the terms we use—the Lakota *tiyospaye*, the Vietnamese *ho*, the Mexican *familia* assert identities of difference that cannot be adequately served by any uniform state-level policy. Despite the fact that American Indians by virtue of their unique federal-trust status receive special mention in the Welfare Reform Act, concomitant concepts of "family" and "work" remain universalized, and render a meaningful application of the legislation impossible to achieve.

The impossibility of successful application of welfare reform rests with its assumptions about individualism, self-sufficiency, family norms, and the cruel ruse that "work" is an automatic antidote to poverty (see Eherenreich 2001; Theriault 1995). This is one reason I was interested in American Indian women's own conceptualizations of work. Despite the overused gloss of "globalization" as a hegemonic and economic process, any understanding of the transnational nature of economic production and exchange should lay to rest revised versions of a self-regulating "moral economy," or the recurring and falsified explanation that poverty is a cultural trait. In wanting to examine contemporary Indigenous conceptions of work, my hope is to move away from popular images of American Indians as discussed in chapter 1 (e.g., from iron-workers to beadworkers) and make room for new voices to emerge, knowingly incomplete, inconsistent, subjective, and ongoing. If welfare reform policies are a backdrop against which people must strategize to make ends meet, then their creativity and innovation becomes a necessary imprint mapped onto the legacy of cultural survival.

Of course not all Indians are poor. Most are urban, and many choose to define their status in other terms altogether, such as Indigenous rejections of federal acknowledgment or renaming as an act of reclaiming. These rejections of colonial impositions speak to the heart of reclamation movements, such as repatriation of cultural properties and the return to Indigenous linguistics (from resurgences in Native American language learning to the retaking of Native American tribal names). In moving away from outmoded anthropological concepts of "adaptation" as a cultural strategy, and the scientism that assigns fixed slots to cultural identity ("traditional" or "progressive"), I suggest that the possibilities for multiple subjectivities allows for greater creative and inventive approaches to work, ceremony, and social life.

Notes

Preface

1. Following from conventional usages, I use the term *American Indian Tribe* to denote those Indigenous groups who now have federal recognition, where *Tribe* designates a governing body.

2. See Wilkinson (1987) and Deloria and Lytle (1983, 1984) for concise overviews of federal Indian policy.

3. The Reverend H. W. Case Collection was bequested to the University of Colorado Museum. Case and his family lived for more than forty years at Fort Berthold, where he founded the First Congregational Church.

4. With a nod to the early reflexive work of Powdermaker's (1966) influential book.

Chapter 1. "Say Commodity Cheese!"

1. Cited in the 1851 Dakota Treaty, article 3.

2. With an increase in intermarriage among whites and the influence of Christianity, evidence suggests an overlapping system of bilaterality, which tends toward more "formal" structures relayed to outsiders—just as American kinship terms have historically entered the kinship nomenclature (e.g., *aunt, uncle, cousin*), but have not replaced traditional modes of reckoning kin.

3. The "*moccasin telegraph*" refers to the informal communication network of gossip and community news.

4. The federal Department of Housing and Urban Development.

5. See the *Mandan, Hidatsa and Arikara Times*, February 25, 1994, for an analysis of internal political disruptions.

6. A cross-cousin is a cousin related to an individual through the individual's mother's brother or through the individual's father's sister.

7. Cited in Berman 1988, 7; originally quoted in the tribal newspaper *Ahead of the Herd* (now the *Mandan, Hidatsa and Arikara Times*), vol. 5, no. 12, 1987.

8. Pronounced "hoshka."

9. The Dawes Severalty Act or General Allotment Act of 1887 divided tribal land holdings into fee-simple property among individual families. The effects of these divisions reverberate today among tribal members, who now, several generations later, sometimes own tracts of family lands in common with various descendants of original allottees.

10. The Shell Creek figure Four Dances gives an account of Bob Tail Bull's ceremonial position that allowed him to assert leadership in the 1864 fission between the Fort Buford and the Fort Berthold Hidatsas. Bowers ([1965] 1993). recorded this account.

Chapter 2. Ceremonial Relations of Production

1. For instance, anthropologist Carol Stack (1975) showed the importance of mutual aid and "swapping" among poor African American women in the urban "flats."

2. Anthroplogist Karen Sacks (1988a) distinguishes between *activists* and *centerpeople*, a term she applies to describe grassroots leadership among African American women organizers in a North Carolina hospital. *Focalwomen* in the context of reservation politics and practices draw more on their kin-based than work-based networks although the two frequently overlap.

3. For a detailed account of the seven clan system see Bowers ([1965] 1992, 124).

4. Following Lowie's (1917) orthography.

5. An "affine" is a relative by marriage.

6. Warbonnet dances are sponsored by a clan relative on the father's side and were originally meant to honor that person.

7. Sororal polygyny is a form of marriage whereby one man marries two or more sisters.

8. The income limit for commodities eligibility was $1,092 per month for a family of three in 1991.

9. Prior to TANF (Temporary Assistance for Needy Families) welfare recipients received AFDC (Aid for Families with Dependent Children).

Chapter 3. Women, Work, and the State

1. Population counts for Fort Berthold vary by roughly 16 percent when compared over time (1982–1992) and between agencies (BIA, State Office of Intergovernmental Assistance, Three Affiliated Tribes Legal Department).

2. From the Treaty of Fort Laramie, September 17, 1851 (Prucha 1975).

3. U.S. Department of Agriculture (DOA) Food and Nutrition Service Newsletter, Fall 1991.

4. Tailgate distribution was among those services threatened by cuts to welfare-based programs through the Welfare Reform Act of 1996.

5. Information on the benefits summarized here was collected prior to welfare reform.

6. This represents 7 to 10 percent of the reservation population.

7. Aid to Families with Dependent Children (AFDC), General Assistance (GA), Personal Responsibility Work Opportunities and Reconciliation Act, Temporary Aid to Needy Families (TANF), Social Security Income (SSI).

8. Maude, an exception to this generalization, tells about her work experience at Northrop in chap. 5.

9. The following section was excerpted in part, and reproduced with permission, from Berman 1996a.

Chapter 4. Mihẻ, Mia, Sǻpat: Women's Ways of Leadership

1. Hidatsa, Mandan and Arikara words for "woman," respectively.

2. Place names and personal names have been changed.

3. For an Indigenous perspective of the conflicts between consensus and majority-vote governance see Wub-e-ke-niew (1995).

4. The cosmological cycle of stories related to the Boy Who Fell to Earth and the Earthnaming Bundle stories associated with the Old Woman Who Never Dies (who is known by several names in English) is recounted in copious detail in Bowers's ([1950] 1991) treatise. What remains of interest here is the power these stories still hold as customary means of asserting cultural legitimacy to place.

5. For an account of the cycle of stories involving the Boy Who Fell to Earth, see Bowers ([1950] 1991).

6. Family names have been changed here to protect potential litigants' identities. Any resemblance to actual family names is only coincidence and not to be taken as factual.

7. Bob Tail Bull gives a detailed account of the split that occurred between the Hidatsa ("river Crow") and the tribe now called "the Crow" (or "mountain Crow") in Bowers ([1965] 1992).

Chapter 5. "All we needed was our gardens . . ." Implications of State Welfare Reform on the Reservation Economy

1. The concept of *reservationization* as put forth by Barbara Buttes embodies the *processes* of dispossession, removal, relocation, and the construction of reservations as communities of containment. I use it here as a way to signal that this process is, by definition, ongoing.

2. With homage to Studs Terkel for setting the stage in *Working*.

3. Manuscript archived at the Fort Berthold Community College Library.

4. The slogan "Carriers of Culture, Bridgebuilders to the Future" was part of the North Dakota NAIWA conference logo emblazoned on t-shirts, tote bags, and conference materials.

5. See Deloria and Lytle (1984). For a legal analysis of the *Marshall* decisions, see Getches and Wilkinson *Federal Indian Law* (1986; 1998).

6. Thanks to Leo Cummings, personal communication. My understandings are completely my own.

7. Three Affiliated Tribes (TAT) Site Visit Report, April 2000.

References

Abromowitz, Mimi. 1988. *Regulating the lives of women: Social welfare policy from colonial times to the present*. Boston: South End Press.

Albers, Patricia. 1983. Sioux women in transition: A study of their changing status in a domestic and capitalist sector of production. In *The hidden half: Studies of Plains Indian women*, edited by Patricia Albers and Beatrice Medicine. New York: University Press of America.

————. 1996. From legend to land to labor: Changing perspectives on Native American work. In *Native Americans and wage labor: Ethnohistorical perspectives*, edited by Alice Littlefield and Martha C. Knack. Norman: University of Oklahoma Press.

Albers, Patricia, and Beatrice Medicine. 1983. *The hidden half: Studies of Plains Indian women*. Lanham, Md.: University Press of America.

Almquist, Elizabeth M. 1986. Further consequences of double jeopardy: The reluctant participation of racial-ethnic women in feminist organizations. In *Ethnicity and women*, edited by Winston A. Van Horne. Milwaukee: University of Wisconsin Press.

Ambler, Maryjane. 1990. *Breaking the iron bonds: Indian control of energy development*. Lawrence: University of Kansas Press.

Anderson, Benedict. 1991. *Imagined communities: Reflections of the origin of nationalism*. London: Vergo Press.

Appadurai, Arjun, ed. 1986. *The social life of things: Commodities in cultural perspective*. Cambridge, England: Cambridge University Press.

Archeluta, Margaret L., Brenda J. Child, and K. Tsianini Lomawaima. 2000. *Away from home: American Indian boarding school experiences. 1879–2000*. Phoenix: Heard Museum; Santa Fe: Museum of New Mexico Press.

Aronowitz, Stanley, and William DiFazio. 1994. *The jobless future: Sci-tech and the dogma of work*. Minneapolis: University of Minnesota Press.

Bahr, Kathleen S., and Howard M. Bahr. 1993. Autonomy, community and the mediation of value: Comments on Apachean grandmothering, culture change and the media. *Family Perspective* 27(4): 347–74.

Baker, Joannemarie, and Teresia Teaiwa. 1994. Enunciating our terms: Women of color in collaboration and conflict. In *Inscriptions* 7: The Center for Cultural Studies. University of California, Santa Cruz: 16–41.

Barry, Norman. 1990. *Welfare*. Minneapolis: University of Minnesota Press.

Basso, Keith. 1996. Wisdom sits in places. In *Senses of Place*, edited by Steven Feld and Keith H. Basso. Santa Fe, N.M.: School of American Research.

Bays, Sharon. 1998. H'mong women's activism in a central California town. In *Community activism and feminist politics: Organizing across race, class and gender*, edited by Nancy Naples. New York: Routledge.

Bell, Diane. 1993. Introduction and Yes, Virginia, there is a feminist ethnography: Reflections from three Australian fields. In *Gendered fields: Women, men and ethnography*, edited by Diane Bell, Pat Caplan, and Wakir Johan Karim. New York: Routledge.

Beneria, Lourdes, and Savitri Bisnath. 2000. Gender and poverty: An analysis for action. In *The globalization reader*, edited by Frank J. Lechner and John Boli. Boston: Blackwell, pp. 172–76.

Beneria, Lourdes, and Sen Gita. 1981. Accumulation, reproduction and women's role in economic development: Boserup revisited. *Signs.* 7 (2): 279–98.

Beneria, Lourdes, and Catherine Stimpson, eds. 1987. *Women, households and the economy*. New Brunswick, NJ: Rutgers University Press.

Berman, Tressa. n.d. Going home: Stories of return migration. Unpublished manuscript.

———. 1988. For the taking: The Garrison Dam and the tribal taking area. *Cultural Survival Quarterly* 12: 5–8.

———. 1989. Hidatsa and Lakota women's arts: Ceremony or commodity? *Anthropology UCLA* 16(2):29–71.

———. 1996a. Bringing it to the center: Artistic production as economic development. In *Research in human capital and development*, Vol. 10, edited by Carol Ward and C. Matthew Snipp, Greenwich, Conn.: JAI Press.

———. 1996b. Hidatsa. In *Encyclopedia of North American Indians: Native American history, culture, and life from Paleo-Indians to the present*, edited by Frederick E. Hoxie. Boston: Houghton Mifflin, pp. 247–48.

————. 1996c. Mandan. In *Encyclopedia of North American Indians: Native American history, culture, and life from Paleo-Indians to the present*, edited by Frederick E. Hoxie. Boston: Houghton Mifflin, pp. 353–54.

———— 1998. The community as worksite: American Indian woman's artistic production. In *More than class studying power in U.S. workplaces*, edited by Anne K. Kingsolver. Albany, N.Y.: State University of New York Press, pp. 73–95.

Biolsi, Thomas. 1993. *Organizing the Lakota*. Tucson: University of Arizona Press.

Biolsi, Thomas, Rose Cordier, Marvine Douville Two Eagle, and Melinda Weil. 2001. Welfare reform on Rosebud reservation: Challenges for tribal policy. Working Paper.

Bohannan, Paul. 1957. *Justice and judgement among the Tiv*. New York: International African Institute, Oxford University Press.

Bolles, Lynn. 1983. Kitchens hit by priorities: Employed working-class Jamaican women confront the IMF. In *Women, men and the international division of labor*, edited by June Nash and Maria Patricia Fernandez-Kelly. Albany, N.Y.: State University of New York Press.

Bookman, Ann, and Sandra Morgen, eds. 1988. *Women and the politics of empowerment*. Philadelphia: Temple University Press.

Bowers, Alfred. [1950] 1991. *Mandan social and ceremonial organization*. Chicago: University of Chicago Press. Reprint, Moscow: University of Idaho Press.

————. [1965] 1992. *Hidatsa social and ceremonial organization*. Bureau of Ethnology Bulletin 194. Washington, D.C.: Smithsonian Institution. Reprint, with an introduction by Douglas Parks, Lincoln: University of Nebraska Press.

Bruner, Edward. 1961. Mandan. *Perspectives in American Indian culture change*, edited by E. H. Spicer. Chicago: University of Chicago Press.

Buttes, Barbara. Forthcoming. *Mdewankanton Dakota women 1860–1900: Oral histories of the early reservation period*.

Bulakishnar, Radhika, ed. 2002. *The hidden assembly line: Gender dynamics of subcontracted work in a global economy*. Bloomfield, Conn.: Kumavarian Press.

Calagione, John. 1992. Working in time: Music and power on the job in New York City. In *Workers' expressions: Beyond accommodation and resistance*, edited by John Calagione, Doris Francis, and Daniel Nugent. Albany, N.Y.: State University of New York Press.

Calagione, John, Doris Francis, and Daniel Nugent, eds. 1992. Worker's expressions: Beyond accommodation and resistance on the margins of capitalism. In *Workers' expressions: Beyond accommodation and resistance*, edited by John Calagione, Doris Francis, and Daniel Nugent. Albany, N.Y.: State University of New York Press.

Canclini, Nestor Garcia. 1994. *Transforming modernity: Popular culture in Mexico*, Translated by Lidia Lozano. Austin: University of Texas Press.

Case, Harold, and Eva Case. 1977. *100 years at Fort Berthold: The history of the Fort Berthold Indian Mission: 1876–1976*. Bismarck Tribune Press.

Champagne, Duane. 1987. American Indian values and the institutionalization of IRA governments. In *American Indian policy and cultural values: Conflict and accommodation*. Los Angeles: American Indian Studies Center.

———. Forthcoming. Will Native American community and identity survive the new economy? *Native Pathways: Economic development and American Indian culture in the twentieth century*. Boulder: University of Colorado Press.

Ching, Barbara, and Gerald W. Creed, eds. 1997. *Knowing your place: Rural identity and cultural hierarchy*. New York: Routledge.

Clark, Blue. 1994. *Lone Wolf v. Hitchock: Treaty rights and the Indian law at the end of the twentieth century*. Lincoln: University of Nebraska Press.

Clifford, James. 1988. *The predicament of culture: Twentieth century ethnography, literature, and art*. Cambridge, Mass.: Harvard University Press.

Clifford, James, and George E. Marcus, eds. 1986. *Writing culture: The poetics and politics of ethnography*. Cambridge, Mass.: Harvard University Press.

Conley, John, M., and William M. O'Barr. 1990. *Rules and relationships: The ethnography of legal discourse*. Chicago: University of Chicago Press.

Cook-Lynn, Elizabeth. 1996. The relationship of a writer to the past. In *Why I can't read Wallace Stegner and other essays: A tribal voice*. Madison: University of Wisconsin Press.

Cornell, Stephen, and Joseph P. Kalt, eds. 1992. *What can tribes do? Strategies and institutions in American Indian economic development*. American Indian Manual and Handbook Series, no. 4. Los Angeles: University of California Press.

———. 2000. We gotta get somethin' *goin'* around here! Paper presented at symposium, Welfare Reform, Job Creation, and American Indian Economies. Empowering American Indian Families: New Perspectives on Welfare Reform, 5–6 May, at Washington University, St. Louis.

Danesh, Abol Hassan. 1999. *Corridor of hope: A visual view of the informal economy*. Lanham, Md.: University Press of America.

Deere, Carmen Diana. 1991. What difference does gender make? Rethinking peasant studies. Gender and Global Issues Lecture Series. Davis: University of California.

Deloria, Philip. 1998. *Playing Indian*. New Haven, Conn.: Yale University Press.

Deloria, Vine, Jr. 1969. *Custer Died for Your Sins: An Indian Manifesto*. Norman: University of Oklahoma Press.

———. 1985. *American Indian policy in the twentieth century*. Norman: University of Oklahoma Press.

Deloria, Vine, Jr., and Clifford Lytle. 1984. *The nations within: The past and future of American Indian sovereignty*. New York: Pantheon.

Deloria, Vine, Jr., and David E. Wilkins. 1999. *Tribes, treaties and constitutional tribulations*. Austin: University of Texas.

di Leonardo, Micaela. 1991. Gender, culture and political economy: Feminist anthropology in historical perspective. In *Gender at the crossroads of knowledge*, edited by Micaela di Leonardo. Berkeley and Los Angeles: University of California Press.

Edelman, Peter. 2002. Reforming welfare-take two. *The Nation*, February 4, 16–20.

Ehrenreich, Barbara. 2001. *Nickel and Dimed: On (not) getting by in America*. New York: Metropolitan Books.

Enloe, Cynthia. 1990. *Bananas, beaches, and bases: Making feminist sense of international politics*. Berkeley and Los Angeles: University of California Press.

Fowler, Loretta. 1987. *Shared symbols, contested meanings: Gros Ventre culture and history, 1778–1984*. Ithaca, N.Y.: Cornell University Press.

Funiciello, Theresa. 1993. *Tyranny of kindness: Dismantling the welfare system to end poverty in America*. New York: Atlantic Monthly Press.

Garrell, Gary. 1992. The curators. *Art News*, September, 73.

Geertz, Clifford. 1988. *Works and lives: The anthropologist as author*. Stanford, Calif.: Stanford University Press.

Getches, David H., Charles F. Wilkson, and Robert A. Williams Jr. 1998. *Cases and materials on federal Indian law*. 4th ed. St. Paul, Minn.: West Group.

Gilkes, Cheryl Townsend. 1988. Building in many places: Multiple commitments and ideologies in black women's community work. In *Women and the politics of empowerment*, edited by Ann Bookman and Sandra Morgen. Philadelphia: Temple University Press.

Gilman, Carolyn, and Mary Jane Schneider. 1987. *The way to independence: Memories of a Hidatsa Indian family, 1840–1920.* Exhibition catalogue. St. Paul: Minnesota Historical Society Press.

Goldberg-Ambrose, Carole. *Planting tail feathers: Tribal survival and Public Law 280.* Los Angeles: American Indian Studies Center, UCLA.

Grewal, Inderpal, and Caren Kaplan, eds. 1994. *Scattered hegemonies: Postmodernity and transnational feminist practices.* Minneapolis: University of Minnesota Press.

Gupta, Akhil, and James Ferguson. 1997. *Culture, power and place.* Durham, N.C.: Duke University Press.

Halbwachs, Maurice. 1992. *On collective memory.* Edited and translated with an Introduction by Lewis Coser. Chicago: University of Chicago Press.

Hanson, Jeffrey R. 1986. Adjustment and adaptation on the Northern Plains: The case of equestrianism among the Hidatsa. *Plains Anthropologist* 31:93–108.

Haraway, Donna. 1988. Situated knowledges: The science question in feminism and the privilege of partial perspective. *Feminist Studies* 14(3):575.

Harvey, Yolanda. (personal communication). White Mountain Apache Tribe Elderly Services.

Hirschwann, Nancy J., and Ulrike Liebert. 2000. *Women and welfare: Theory and practice in the U.S. and Europe.* New Brunswick, N.J.: Rutgers University Press.

Hirsh, B. 1991. American Indian Child Welfare Act, the next ten years: Indian homes for Indian children. In *American Indian child welfare: Unto the seventh generation conference proceedings*, edited by Troy Johnson. Los Angeles: University of California, American Indian Research Center.

hooks, bell. 1994. *Outlaw culture: Resisting representations.* New York: Routledge.

Hyde, Lewis. 1989. *The gift. Imagination and the erotic life of property.* New York: Vintage Books.

Jaimes, Annette, and Theresa Halsey. 1992. American Indian women: At the center of Indigenous resistance in North America. In *The state of Native America: Genocide, colonization, and resistance*, edited by M. Annette Jaimes. Boston: South End Press, pp. 311–44.

Johnson, Troy. 1993. The Indian Child Welfare Act: Unto the seventh generation. Proceedings of conference held 15–17 January, University of California at Los Angeles, Faculty Center.

Jojola, Ted. 1973. Memoirs of an American Indian house; U.S. federally subsidized Indian housing. Master's thesis, School of City Planning, Department of Urban Studies and Planning, Massachusetts Institute of Technology, Cambridge.

Jones, A. Wesley. Personal communication with author.

Jordan, June. 1992. Don't you talk about my momma! In *Technical difficulties: African American notes on the state of the union*. New York: Pantheon, pp. 65–80.

Kaplan, Caren, Norma Alarcón, and Minoo Moallem, eds. 1999. *Between women and nation: Nationalism, transnational feminisms and the state*. Durham, N.C.: Duke University Press.

Karp, Ivan, and Steven D. Lavine. 1991. *Exhibiting cultures: The poetics and politics of museum display*. Washington, D.C.: Smithsonian Institution Press.

Keith, Michael, and Steve Pile, eds. 1993. *Place and the politics of identity*. London: Routledge.

Kemnitzer, Luis. Personal communication with author.

Kemnitzer, Luis, William Willard, et al. 1971. Urban Indian Relocation Study. Mimeograph manuscript archived at San Francisco State University. Unpublished manuscript National Institute of Mental Health.

Klein, Alan. 1980. Plains economic analyses: The Marxist complement. In *Anthropology on the Great Plains*, edited by W. Raymond Wood and Margo Liberty. Lincoln: University of Nebraska Press.

———. 1983. The Plains truth: The impact of colonialism on Indian women. *Dialectical Anthropology* 7:299–313.

Lamphere, Louise. 1977. *To run after them: Cultural and social bases of cooperation in a Navajo community*. Albuquerque: University of New Mexico Press. Reprint, Tucson: University of Arizona Press.

———. 1987. *From working mothers to working daughters: Immigrant women in a New England industrial community*. Ithaca, N.Y.: Cornell University Press.

Lawson, Michael L. [1982] 1994. *Damned Indians. The Pick-Sloan Plan and the Missouri [1994] River Sioux*. Norman: University of Oklahoma Press. Revised with a foreword by Vine Deloria, Jr.

Leacock, Eleanor. 1978. Women's status in egalitarian societies. *Current Anthropology* 19(2):247–55.

Leeper Buss, Fran. 1985. *Dignity: Lower income women tell of their lives and struggles*. Ann Arbor: University of Michigan Press.

Lewis, Oscar. 1961. *The children of Sanchez: Autobiography of a Mexican family*. New York: Random House.

Lieder, Michael. 1993. Navajo dispute resolution and promissory obligations: Continuity and change in the Navajo Nation. *American Indian Law Review* 18 (1):1–71.

Littlefield, Alice, and Martha C. Knack, eds. 1996. *Native Americans and wage labor: Ethnohistorical perspectives*. Norman: University of Oklahoma Press.

Lobo, Susan. 1990/1992. Oakland's American Indian community: History, social organization and factors that contribute to census undercounts. Washington, D.C.: Center for Survey Methods Resources Bureau of the Census.

Lobo, Susan, and Kurt Peters, eds. 2001. *American Indians and the urban experience*. Walnut Creek, Calif.: AltaMira Press.

Lomawaima, Tsianina. 1994. *They called it prairie light: The story of Chilocco Indian school*. Lincoln: University of Nebraska Press.

Lowie, Robert H. 1917. Notes on the social organization and customs of the Mandan-Hidatsa and Crow. New York: American Museum of Natural History Anthropological Papers, vol. 21, pt. 1.

MacKinnon, Catherine A. 1987. *Feminism unmodified: Discourses in life and law*. Cambridge, Mass.: Harvard University Press.

Malouf, Carl. 1963. Crow-Flies-High Village site 32MZ1, River Basin Survey, Bureau of American Ethnology bulletin report. Washington, DC: Smithsonian Institution.

March, Kathryn S., and Taqqu, Rachelle L. 1986. *Women's informal associations in developing countries*. Boulder, Colo.: Westview Press.

Marcus, George F., and Michael M. J. Fischer. 1986. *Anthropology as cultural critique*. Chicago: University of Chicago Press.

Marx, Karl. 1867. *Das kapital (Capital)*. Vol. 1 of *The Marx-Engels Reader*, 2nd ed., edited by Robert Tucker. New York: Norton.

Massey, Doreen. 1994. *Space, place and gender*. New York: Polity Press.

Mauss, Marcel. [1923] 1967. *The gift: Forms and functions of exchange in archaic societies*. Translated by Ian Cunnison. *Essai sur le don: Forme et raison de l'echange dans les societés archaiques. L'Année Sociologique* I (1923–24).

McLaughlin, Irene Castle. 1992. The politics of agricultural decline on the Fort Berthold Indian reservation, North Dakota. *Culture and Agriculture*, Fall Issue, no. 44.

———. 1993. Colonialism, cattle and class: A century of ranching on the Fort Berthold Indian reservation. Ph.D. diss., Columbia University, New York.

Medicine, Beatrice. 1986. Contemporary cultural revitalization: Bilingual and cultural education. *Wicazo Sa Review: American Indian Studies Journal* 2(1):31–35.

———. 1993. North American Indigenous women and cultural domination. *American Indian Culture and Research Journal* 17(3):121–30.

Meyer, Roy W. 1977. *The Village Indians of the Upper Missouri: The Mandans, Hidatsas and Arikaras*. Lincoln: University of Nebraska Press.

Mink, Gwendolyn. 1999. *Whose welfare?* Ithaca, N.Y.: Cornell University Press.

Moore, John H. 1996. The significance of Cheyenne work in the history of U.S. capitalism. In *Native Americans and wage labor: Ethnohistorical perspectives*, edited by Alice Littlefield and Martha C. Knack. Norman: University of Oklahoma Press.

Moroney, Robert, and Judy Krysik. 1998. *Social policy and social work: Critical essays on the welfare state*. New York: de Gruyter.

Moynihan, Daniel Patrick. 1965. The Negro family: The case for national action. Washington, D.C.: U.S. Government Printing Office. Prepared for the Office of Policy Planning and Research for the Department of Labor.

Naples, Nancy. 1998. *Grassroots warriors: Activist mothering, community work, and the war on Poverty*. New York: Routledge.

Nash, June. 1993. *Crafts in the world market: The impact of global exchange on Middle American artisans*. Albany, N.Y.: State University of New York Press.

Nash, June, and Maria Patricia Fernandez-Kelly, eds. 1983. *Women, men and the international division of labor*. Albany, N.Y.: State University of New York Press.

Nirayan, Kirin. 1993. How native is a "Native" anthropologist? *American Anthropologist* 95:671–86.

O'Brien, Sharon. 2000. Traditional values and the administration of welfare reform. Paper presented at symposium, Empowering American Indian Families: New Perspectives on Welfare Reform, 5–6 May, at Washington University, St. Louis.

Ong, Aihwa. 1987. *Spirits of resistance and capitalist discipline: Factory women in Malaysia*. Albany, N.Y.: State University of New York Press.

Orchard, William C. 1971. *The technique of porcupine quill decoration among the North American Indians*. New York: Museum of the American Indian, Heye Foundation.

Pandit, Kavita, and Suzanne Davies Withers, eds. 1999. *Migration and restructuring in the United States: A geographic perspective*. Lanham, Md.: Rowman and Littlefield.

Pandy, S., E. F. Brown, Min Zhan, Shannon Collier, and Kathryn Hui. 1999. Promise of welfare reform development through devolution on Indian reservations. *Journal of Poverty* 3(4):37–61.

———. 2000. *How are families on reservations faring under welfare reform?* St. Louis: Washington University, George Warren Brown School of Social Work.

Peters, Kurt. 1995. Santa Fe Cam, House 21, Richmond, California: Persistence of identity among Laguna Pueblo laborers, 1945–1982. *American Indian Culture and Research Journal* 19(3):71–85.

———. 2001. Continuing identity: Laguna Pueblo railroaders in Richmond, California. In *American Indians and the Urban Experience*, edited by Susan Lobo and Kurt Peters. Walnut Creek, Calif.: AltaMira Press.

Pickering, Kathleen Ann. 2000. *Lakota Culture, World Economy*. Lincoln: University of Nebraska Press.

Piven, Frances Fox. 1995. Foreword to *Words of welfare: The poverty of social science and the social science of poverty*, by Sanford F. Schram. Minneapolis: University of Minnesota Press.

Piven, Frances Fox, and Richard Clowen. 1971. *Regulating the poor: The functions of public welfare*. New York: Pantheon.

Polanyi, Karl. 1944. *The great transformation*. New York: Farrar & Rinehart.

Pommershein, Frank. 1995. *Braid of feathers: American Indian law and contemporary tribal life*. Berkeley and Los Angeles: University of California Press.

Powdermaker, Hortense. 1966. *Stranger and friend, the way of an anthropologist*. New York: Norton.

Powers, Marla N. 1986. *Oglala women. Myth, ritual and reality*. Chicago: University of Chicago Press.

Prucha, Francis Paul. 1975. *Documents of United States Indian policy*. Reprint, Lincoln: University of Nebraska Press.

Quadagno, Jill. 1994. *The color of welfare: How racism undermined the war on poverty*. New York: Oxford University Press.

Red Horse, John. 1988. Cultural evolution of American Indian families. In *Ethnicity and race*, edited by C. Jacobs and D. Bowles. Silver Springs, Md.: National Association of Social Workers.

Reifel, Ben. 1952. Relocation of the Fort Berthold Indian reservation. Ph.D. diss., Harvard University, Cambridge.

Rodriguez, Jessie. 1990. The black community and the birth control movement. In *Unequal sisters: A multicultural reader in U.S. women's history*, edited by Ellen Carol Dubois and Vicki L. Ruiz. London: Routledge.

Rogers, J. Daniel. 1990. *Objects of change*. Washington, D.C.: Smithsonian Institution Press.

Rosaldo, Renato. 1993. *Culture and truth*. Stanford, Calif.: Stanford University Press.

Sacks, Karen Brodkin. 1988a. *Caring by the hour*. Chicago: University of Illinois Press.

———. 1988b. Gender and grassroots leadership. In *Women and the politics of empowerment*, edited by Ann Bookman and Sandra Morgen. Philadelphia: Temple University Press.

———. 1989. Toward a unified theory of race, class and gender. *American Ethnologist* 16(3):534–50.

Sahlins, Marshall. 1972. *Stone Age economics*. Chicago: Aldine Atherton.

Schneider, Mary Jane. 1981. Economic aspects of Mandan/Hidatsa giveaways. *Plains Anthropologist* 26(91):43–50.

———. 1980. Plains Indian art. In *Anthropology on the Great Plains*, edited by W. Raymond Wood and Margot Liberty. Lincoln: University of Nebraska Press.

Schraeder, Robert Fay. 1983. *American Indian arts and crafts board: An aspect of New Deal policy*. Albuquerque: University of New Mexico Press.

Schram, Sanford F. 1995. *Words of welfare: The poverty of social science and the social science of poverty*. Minneapolis: University of Minnesota Press.

Scott, James C. 1990. *Domination and the arts of resistance: Hidden transcripts*. New Haven, Conn.: Yale University Press.

———. 1998. *Seeing like a state: How certain schemes to improve the human condition have failed*. New Haven, Conn.: Yale University Press.

Sheffield, Gail. 1997. *The arbitrary Indian: The Indian Arts and Craft Act of 1990*. Norman: University of Oklahoma Press.

Spector, Janet. 1983. What this awl means: Feminist archaeology at a Wahpeton Dakota village. St. Paul: Minnesota Historical Society Press.

Stack, Carol B. 1975. *All our kin: Strategies for survival in a black community*. New York: Harper and Row.

Stacey, Judith. 1990. *Brave new families*. New York: Bantam Books.

———. 1997. Beyond what are given as givens: Ethnography and critical policy studies. *Ethos* 25(2):191–207.

Stilman, Janet. 1987. *Enough is enough: Aboriginal women speak out*. Ottawa, Ont.: Women's Press.

Stoller, Paul. 1996. Spaces, places, and fields: The politics of West African trading in New York City's informal economy. *American Anthropologist* 98(4):776.

Strickland, Rennard. 1998. The eagle's empire: Sovereignty, survival and self-governance in Native American law and constitutionalism. In *Studying Native American Problems and Prospects*, edited by R. Thornton. Madison: University of Wisconsin Press.

Stromwall, Layne K. Bruzy, Polly Sharp, and Celina Anderson. 1988. The implications of "welfare reform" for American Indian families and communities. In *Pressing issues of inequality and American Indian Communities*, edited by Elizabeth Segal and Keith M. Kilty. Binghamton, N.Y.: Haworth Press.

Sutton, Imre. 2000. The continuing saga of Indian land claims. *American Indian Culture and Research Journal* 24(1):129–62.

Taussig, Michael T. 1980. *The devil and commodity fetishism*. Chapel Hill: University of North Carolina Press.

Taylor, Christopher. 1992. *Milk, honey and money*. Washington, D.C.: Smithsonian Institution Press.

Terkel, Studs. 1974. *Working; People talk about what they do all day and how they feel about what they do*. New York: Pantheon Books.

Teski, Marea C., and Jacob J. Climo, eds. 1995. *The labyrinth of memory: Ethnographic journeys*. Westport, Conn.: Bergin and Garvey.

Theriault, Reg. 1995. *How to tell when you're tired. A brief examination of work*. New York: Norton.

Trinh, T. Minh-Ha. 1989. *Woman Native Other: Writing postcoloniality and feminism*. Bloomington: Indiana University Press.

Tsing, Anna Lowenhaupt. 1993. *In the realm of the diamond queen: Marginality in an out-of-the-way place.* Princeton, N.J.: Princeton University Press.

Turner, Victor. 1982. *Celebration: Studies in festivity and ritual.* Washington, D.C.: Smithsonian Institution Press.

Walker, Alice. 1994. Everyday use. In *Love and Trouble: Stories of Black Women.* Edited and with an introduction by Barbara Christian. New Brunswick, N.J.: Rutgers University Press.

Ward, Carol, and C. Matthew Snipp. 1996. American Indian economic development. In *Research in human capital and development,* edited by Carol Ward and Matthew Snipp. Greenwich, Conn.: JAI Press.

Weiner, Annette B. 1992. *Inalienable possessions: The paradox of keeping-while-giving.* Berkeley and Los Angeles: University of California Press.

Weiss, Lawrence David. 1984. *The development of capitalism in the Navajo Nation.* Minneapolis, Minn.: Marxist Educational Press.

Weist, Katherine M. 1983. Plains Indian women. In *Anthropology on the Great Plains,* edited by W. Raymond Wood and Margot Liberty. Lincoln: University of Nebraska Press.

Wellman, David. 1996. Red and black and white America: Discovering cross-border identities and other subversive activities. In *Names we call home: Autobiography on racial identity,* edited by Becky Thompson and Sangeeta Tyagi. New York: Routledge.

White, James Boyd. 1990. *Justice as translation: An essay in cultural and legal criticism.* Chicago: University of Chicago Press.

Wilkins, David. 1997. *American Indian sovereignty and the U.S. Supreme Court: The masking of justice.* Austin: University of Texas Press.

Wilkins, David, and Tsianini Lomawaima. 2001. *Uneven ground: American Indian sovereignty and federal law.* Norman: University of Oklahoma Press.

Wilkinson, Charles F. 1987. *American Indians, time and the law: Native societies in modern constitutional democracy.* New Haven, Conn.: Yale University Press.

Wilson, Gilbert L. [1914] 1985. *Goodbird the Indian.* Introduction by Mary Jane Schneider. St. Paul: Minnesota Historical Society Press.

———. [1917] 1985. *Buffalo Bird Woman's garden.* Introduction by Jeffrey Hanson. St. Paul: Minnesota Historical Society Press.

Index